Schoolmaking

Schoolmaking

An Alternative in Teacher Education

Carolyn Lipton Ellner
Claremont Graduate School

B.J. Barnes
California State University,
Fullerton

Lexington Books
D.C. Heath and Company
Lexington, Massachusetts
Toronto

Library of Congress Cataloging in Publication Data

Ellner, Carolyn Lipton.
   Schoolmaking.

   Includes index.
   1. Teachers, Training of. 2. Education—Experimental methods.
3. Laboratory schools. 4. Educational innovations. I. Barnes, Betty J.,
joint author. II. Title.
LB1715.E5   370'.7122   77-2679
ISBN 0-669-01626-8

Published simultaneously in Canada

Printed in the United States of America

International Standard Book Number: 0-669-01626-8

Library of Congress Catalog Card Number: 77-2679

to our children and theirs

Contents

Preface

In addition to giving the reader some idea of what a book is about, we believe a preface should also suggest what will *not* be found between its covers. The reader *will* find here an account of a two-year experimental program in teacher education. The essence of this program is an adventure in schoolmaking that engaged and challenged fourteen young people determined to become teachers who could change things. This adventure resulted in six little schools. Operated during the summer between the two years, each school provided a unique opportunity to experiment with the process of schooling and to learn from it.

Because *Schoolmaking* is a study of an experimental program in teacher education, the reader might expect to find its pages filled with statistical analyses. Not so. There is not a multiple regression table in the book! Numbers do not yield the kind of "truth" we are seeking.

While we are not primarily counters of data, we do carefully examine and analyze them to raise important questions about processes of education, from preschool to graduate school. If the issues we deal with seem as critical to the reader as they do to us, perhaps the study will have contributed to a vision of schooling and its potential to affect the quality of life in the United States of America. What readers see in the book will depend mostly upon the level at which the book is read. It is a case study of real persons whose names are fictitious. It will mean different things to different people.

Schoolmaking is the story of a program in which we, the storytellers, were deeply immersed. We were both participants and observers. We were involved professionally and personally with the program participants, and we want to involve the reader also. For us, professionalism implies personalism and personalism takes account of *meaning*.

The meaning to people of any experience does not begin with the experience, nor does it end with it. Therefore, the book begins with "the times" from which both the participants' commitments and the program emerged. It describes the program, the participants, and the effects each had upon the other. Outcomes are described in the chapters on the minischools.

But the book does not end with an ad hoc evaluation of these "culminating experiences." It revisits the program five years later by revisiting the participants. They are asked not only how they felt about it at the time, but they are questioned about how the program seemed to them after they had taught for a while. They are asked about the way it has affected their lives, and what they think about it in relation to the kinds of persons—"professionals"—they have become. The book ends with an attempt to answer the question: "What does all of this mean?" Each reader's answer to this question will also contribute to the ultimate promise of the book.

The central premise of the program was that things don't just happen to people, but that people can be effective agents in making things happen. The program was intended to contribute to the development of such people—change agents—or "teacher leaders." If the book has reported upon that process with a measure of truth, it will have achieved a major purpose. Additionally, if the questions raised impel a reader to action, the book will have counted *for* a great deal.

Who are these potential readers with the power to make things happen? They are people who influence educational processes at three levels: instructional, institutional, and societal.[a] At the instructional level are aspiring teachers, as well as practitioners and teacher educators. Both preservice and inservice teachers should find in the minischool experiences many concrete examples of classroom practices worth noting. They may wish to critique them, enlarge upon them, and even adapt them for their own classrooms.

The book may be read at a second level by persons who represent institutions. At this institutional level are school administrators, staff developers, professors of education, as well as people in other fields who are concerned with social behavior and human organization. School district central office personnel, as well as principals, program coordinators, and curriculum developers, should find new ideas that could serve as models for modification and local development.

The minischool concept may be studied for its applicability to the preservice or continuing education of teachers by the institutions responsible for doing this. The study provides material for seminar discussion and analysis. Students of behavior and of social relationships within the academic community might be stimulated to consider critical issues suggested by the case study and hence be guided toward the theoretical or empirical investigation of related matters.

Among readers at the third or societal level are concerned citizens interested in social change directed toward cultural democracy. Policymakers also will read at this level, as will many general readers who are simply interested in education. "Concerned citizens" are often looking for problems requiring attention. They look, too, for indicators that suggest the directions in which solutions might be found. Whether such persons express themselves through organized efforts or solely at the ballot box, the book may be helpful. Policymakers, on the other hand, rarely have to look for problems. They are confronted with them—in offices, board rooms, and at the bargaining table. Their need is for new perspectives. The book could help in the search for such perspectives.

The purposes of the "general reader" are not as easily identified as those of the other types of readers mentioned above. But one thing we believe: The general reader shares with us all, both readers and writers, the opportunity for a thought-provoking engagement with an interesting group of schoolmakers—the fourteen participants who people its pages and thereby bring abstract concepts to life.

---

[a]We are indebted to John Goodlad who initially introduced this construct to the authors.

Acknowledgments

We would like to thank those persons at the Claremont Graduate School whose encouragement meant something special to us because of their judgment and competence. Their support sustained us throughout an enterprise that seemed to take longer than we could have imagined. Barnaby Keeney, former CGS president, is not given to gratuitous words, much less praise. So when, after reading part of our manuscript, he volunteered that we might have something "significant," we were sustained for at least another six months. We know that he read it because we found little green garden gnats between its pages when he returned it to us. Donald McNassor, former chairman of the Faculty in Education, encouraged and helped us while he was alive, and his memory has continued to inspire us. Malcolm Douglass has been a good personal and professional friend to us both. In fact we were fortunate to have been surrounded by colleagues who stimulated, questioned, and challenged us.

Professional colleagues from other institutions also lent support. Significant among these were Bruce Joyce of Stanford University, William A. Lucio of UCLA, and Robert Stout of California State University, Fullerton. As our manuscript neared completion, John Hogan of the Rand Corporation read it, believed in it, and guided *Schoolmaking* through the publishing wilderness.

The schoolmakers themselves have put up with a lot. When they entered the program, they had not bargained for seven years of questions and correspondence. We value their help individually and as a group, and we regret that their identities must remain anonymous for they have given us insight and perspective. We believe they have also given something to a new generation of teachers.

Those who helped us prepare the manuscript made an immense contribution. Jean Russell and Melanie Komendat typed early drafts. Ethel McKenzie completed the project with dedicated enthusiasm, having adopted it as her own.

While many authors are able to acknowledge the work of spouses on their manuscripts, our husbands cannot type. This does not in any way diminish the importance of their contributions to *Schoolmaking*. Their patience and caring are resources upon which we continually draw.

**Part I
The Challenge Of Change**

1 The Challenge to Change

In the summer of 1971 fourteen untested and aspiring teachers created six community-based vacation schools.[a] They accomplished tasks few experienced educators would have undertaken without trepidation. Perhaps their lack of experience in traditional schooling with its conventional assumptions about what a school should be helped them. On the other hand, perhaps it was too great a familiarity with the conventional wisdom and the boredom and apathy that have often resulted from it. Whatever the subtle influences were that moved and sustained the group, the prospective teachers created unique educational enterprises. To walk through the door of one of these schools was to experience a charge of hope. That electrical quality which communicates involvement in learning seemed a good indicator that these schools-for-one-summer were better adapted to the needs of the communities they served than were many institutions among their established counterparts. These adventures in schoolmaking were part of an experiment in teacher education at the graduate level. The outcomes reported here suggest compelling alternatives to practices current among teacher training programs.

The six enterprises were dubbed "minischools" because they were never intended to be other than *little* schools that operated within a small community and for only a short time. The "mini" budget that gave them substance and sustenance insured that, like the proverbial shoestring, they would have not only a beginning, but also an end. The life-support system of each minischool was strong and functional, and it was limited. It was limited by the primary purpose behind the minischools: teaching teachers to teach—differently.

The experimental program that culminated in the minischools had a purpose beyond their establishment. It was designed to foster among new teachers the awareness and the understanding that are required when planning for change. An assumption upon which the design rested was that the program participants, armed with a broad perspective, would come to possess increased decision-making ability. With consciousness thus heightened, the new teachers were expected to have significant impact upon the institutions of which they would become a part. The minischools they created were intended to involve them in decision making and to test their organizational and instructional skills. In their

---

[a]Of fifteen program participants, fourteen implemented the minischools and completed the program. One left Southern California in order to teach children in a remote village of Mexico.

3

minischools they could continue to grow in these dimensions. Beyond merely producing new teachers, the program was designed to produce a new kind of teacher: a "teacher leader" who would be an agent of institutional change.

In a sense, teachers in this country have always been regarded as agents of change. The United States has institutionalized change,[1] and it has relied upon institutions, especially schools, to effect national growth and development. Paradoxically, however, schools, along with other institutions, have tended to become conservative influences. While historically this conservatism has often been cause for concern, today the problem is critical.

As the nation moves into its third century, its social institutions, including its schools, are on a collision course with the future. Social innovation has not caught up to technological advancement, and the breach is one that has been tearing at the fabric of our society. Pollution, unemployment, and intergroup tensions are just some of the problems that seem to have been exacerbated by technical change. This country's leadership in technological development has made it the first to experience the trauma that accompanies change.[2]

In some ways we are well equipped to deal with the problems facing us: The heterogeneity of American society suggests that we possess resources for generating a variety of solutions from which we might choose. On the other hand, the opportunity that is suggested by these options holds potential for divisiveness as traditional values and institutions are challenged. A homogeneous society would not be as seriously threatened in this way, nor would an engineered society. In some way we must plan for new challenges and for unforeseen conditions.

Planning *for* change is not the same as "planned change." Planned change implies that the ends may be identified and that progress toward achieving these ends may be ascertained in measurable terms.[3] With known ends and with objectives sequenced in a logically staged order, planned change requires only that a ground plan be followed for achievement of the goal. The system is mechanical—that is, linear and engineered for specific outcomes. As such, it is well adapted to an industrial society and to a standardized product. A closed system is inappropriate, however, for a pluralistic society. In a postindustrial era, diversity may prove to be a means for human survival as well as human enrichment. Today especially, the United States needs teachers prepared to consider alternatives to the industrial model.

One alternative approach is to plan for change without identifying the specific outcomes to be obtained. Planning *for* change requires fluidity and adaptability. Planners must acknowledge the dynamic nature of social processes as well as a multiplicity of goals. These are rarely definable in clear and precise terms when a complex tangle of issues and problems is confronted. Rather than being susceptible to orderly reproduction by strict adherence to a ground plan, the alternative to planned change develops as a unique, yet ongoing response to a specific situation. With an emphasis on process, the alternative is closer to an ecological or metabolic model than to an engineered or mechanical one. Risk is inherent in this process.

The inhabitants of a pluralistic society must learn to exercise constant vigilance and openness to the possibilities that reside in the unknown. They lack the security of the closed industrial model in which members of the system may be likened to interchangeable parts. The problems they confront are not likely to respond to catalogue-item solutions; rather, such problems must be approached clinically. With this approach, tolerance for ambiguity becomes necessary and is valued because results may not be easily controlled.

Open systems require open-minded people who, when confronted with multi-dimensional problems, do not seek single-track solutions. To serve a pluralistic society adequately, its institutions, including schools, must be open to new and untried options. Its educational system, therefore, must be supported by teachers who are not socialized into the norms and values of the existing system, but who can find new ways of attacking both old and new problems.

During the more than forty years from Waller[4] to Lortie,[5] research into the socialization of teachers has produced similar evidence: New teachers become like old teachers.[6] The student teaching process, which is almost a universal part of teacher preparation, seems to bear a heavy responsibility for these outcomes.[7] The minischool component of the Teacher Leader Program was an attempt to find an alternative to the usual apprentice-type involvement in which the neophyte is given a subordinate role within a dyadic relationship. Minischools were learning experiences directed toward opening up alternative role behaviors rather than narrowing the number of options available to a teacher.

The program was implemented following the tumultuous events of "the sixties" when it became particularly apparent that change was needed within and among the nation's institutions. During this decade, a large measure of attention and hope became focused upon the schools as instruments of social justice. Ambitious government-supported projects were enthusiastically conceived and were launched to meet the need for educational innovation. The "Program to Develop Teacher Leaders Specializing in the Problems of the Disadvantaged,"[8] which got underway in 1970, was perhaps the last of its genre.[9] It was the beneficiary of funds that were left over from the War on Poverty.

The discrepancy between traditional American ideals and progress toward their realization for certain segments of society had, during the sixties, wrought dissatisfaction with institutionalized solutions, which in turn resulted in disaffection toward the established society. Efforts to peacefully achieve justice, social progress, and participatory democracy were frequently aborted. The nation became familiar with terror in its cities and violence in its schools. Efforts to make the poor and the powerless more vital forces in society seemed to have negligible effect when compared with the enormity of the problem.

While there were some attempts at peaceful, evolutionary change, the process was slow and ponderous. It often resulted in illusory promises and subsequent disillusionment. Still, Americans continued to place their trust in schooling as an instrument of mobility. Its impact during an era marked by increasing restlessness and alienation was less than dramatic, however. Those internal structures that had been developed—such as middle schools, nongrading, team teaching, and early childhood education programs—were used as palliatives to those seeking change. New combinations of old ingredients and fresh labels appealed to a contemporary taste for change. They did not, however, significantly alter the essential content or texture of educational fare.

Although alternatives to educational programs are desirable for all children, traditional structures and methods did not appear to have significantly impeded children of the dominant, white, middle class. Through their behavior and the values that permeate their existence, these children traditionally gained access to economic and social opportunity.[10] Poor and culturally different children did not have such positive determinants working for them, however. Ways of helping such children achieve rich, fulfilling, and productive lives were sought with increasing urgency. More educators came to understand that the anguish and helplessness of poverty which created a self-perpetuating cycle, had made this goal unattainable in the past. The nation's schools by being party to the process had contributed to the disenfranchisement and alienation of large segments of its citizenry.

Following widespread civil disorders, considerable federal legislation was aimed at effecting educational change. The government played an increasingly active role in developing new approaches and exploring new concepts. The vision was to eliminate family income, race, and physical and mental handicaps as impediments to equal educational opportunity.[11]

Despite a massive free system of public schooling, educators had clearly failed to develop strategies that would enable schools to serve all children. Methods, materials, and expectations had become entrenched in routinized norms, which subtly pressured neophyte teachers into conformity.[12] Socialized into the value structure of the middle class[13] and into the mindlessness of schools,[14] teachers generally had little impact on making the schools instruments of upward mobility or even instruments of literacy for a large portion of the population. Instead of adjusting institutions to meet the needs of people who were not or could not be reached through traditional educational methods and organizational patterns, educators blamed the failure of the schools on the shortcomings of students. Teachers' attitudes toward students were discovered to be especially influential in the process of determinism through expectation. In the findings of one study, nearly all the variability in learning among a low-income student population was attributed to teacher expectation.[15]

During the 1960s numerous commissions and conferences provided evidence that change was needed. The Coleman Report showed that teacher quality had greater effect on educational achievement than did facilities and curriculum.[16] Later, the Research and Policy Committee of the Committee for Economic

Development, summarizing massive data, concluded that the achievement of minority group students especially stood in direct relationship to the abilities and preparation of teachers.[17]

While early compensatory programs were based on a hypothesis of deficiency[18] within students, later emphasis was placed upon the cultural *differences* between students' homes and the characteristics of schools. A variety of research projects throughout the country were charged with bridging the gap—that is, with developing materials, programs, and strategies that matched identified characteristics of disadvantaged groups. The specifications for implementing many U.S. Office of Education–sponsored projects and programs suggested the importance of linking them to the culture of local communities. Such linkage was often attempted through the development of new "teacher proof" materials and by employing paraprofessionals familiar with the values and language of the schools' clientele. However, until the last quarter of the decade most of the experiments in education that burgeoned in the sixties were concerned with mechanisms at the public school level: changing classrooms and buildings in structure and relationships; lowering student-teacher ratios; obtaining special equipment, new materials, and instructional aides; and fostering community involvement.

Increasingly, however, the fact became apparent that the attempts to make schools more relevant to the powerless neglected to consider the influence of that person most central to their success or failure: the teacher. In the late sixties the teacher's role within the school-community milieu was finally acknowledged as a critical element in any program's success. Educators looking to eradicate patterns of failure recognized that teachers were needed who understood the social as well as the psychological processes involved in planning for change. The Teacher Leader Program was developed with government support in response to this recognized need.

This volume is an effort to describe and evaluate the project. The Teacher Leader Program was multifaceted and thus reflected a broad spectrum of objectives at many levels. These were associated with its general purpose: to develop a cadre of competent, courageous persons willing to assume leadership roles in a changing world. Many program and participant objectives were achieved through the minischools. These are explained herein, along with descriptions of each of the minischool programs.

Besides functioning as individual educational experiments, the minischool experiences served to hone and to test the potential teachers' abilities. The projects required them to assess needs, establish objectives, make administrative and curricular decisions, and implement and evaluate programs. Many outcomes were immediately apparent and were of themselves instructive. Others, which pertained to the enduring usefulness of the minischool experiences, required time to test. In addition to examining the multidimensional thrust of the program at the time it was in process, this study takes a longitudinal perspective.

The participants were contacted five years later in order to determine the program's long-range effects upon them.

One experiment in teacher preparation can hardly be expected to bring about the educational changes required by globally changing conditions. It can only suggest alternatives to consider. After seven years there are significant findings to report about the teachers who engaged in the schoolmaking experiment. They are different from others who had not met this challenge.

Part II
Responding to the Challenge

2 The Program

Teachers with different attitudes and methods had to be produced if changes in schooling were to be made. In 1970, the tumultuous events of the preceding decade clearly suggested the urgency of this need for change. The first priority for teacher preparation institutions, therefore, was to find new ways of helping teachers to help children. Teachers needed to be equipped with new understandings, skills, and strategies if they were to be creative and influential persons with the power to affect the lives of youngsters positively.

In response to this challenge, the Office of Teacher Education at the Claremont Graduate School developed an experimental alternative program of teacher preparation. It was intended to produce a cadre of change agents. Six "little schools" were the fruit of this project, which consisted of a preservice year, the minischool summer, and a year of salaried and supervised internship in the public schools. During the period that preceded their employment as interns, the participants were known as "preterns."

The program's objectives and design were based upon a recognized need for creative teachers who are able to assume leadership roles in the educational process. From traditional teacher training programs, new teachers are produced who are quickly socialized into the teaching profession to become indistinguishable from teachers who have been members of the profession for ten or twenty years or more. Underlying the program's structure was a belief that if innovating behavior is to be facilitated, new ways of preparing teachers must be found.

The Teacher Leader Program focused upon developing in its participants the flexibility, the competence, and the power to effect changes in relation to the educational circumstances of poor and culturally different children. It adopted as its mission the preparation of superior teachers who would provide leadership in education and who would have special skills for working with other than the dominant culture. Armed with an understanding of the schools' clientele, such teachers would be able to make those informed decisions that are necessary if the schools are to become less remote and alien to the poor and the different. These newly trained professionals would help the schools become places where learning takes place because they would be responsive to people's needs and aspirations. Such schools would serve as instruments of cultural democracy and would be resources to communities—that is, resources people could use and trust because of their involvement in the process.

The education of teachers such as these—teachers dedicated to empowering the powerless—would ultimately ensure that the schools in ghettos and barrios

11

would not be staffed by marginal or indifferent teachers but by persons with a conscious commitment to working in these areas. Such preparation would produce vigorous advocates of educational change. These advocates would speak not as eager laymen or dilettantes but as professionals able to conceive of alternatives to existing structures—that is, as professionals with the knowledge and skill necessary to explore alternatives in order that schools might become healthy, vigorous, and productive.

The program was designed to accomplish a number of purposes congruent with the philosophy of evolutionary change. First, it was intended to develop teachers who would act as generators of new ideas and who would be ready to examine and consider new solutions for both old and new problems. Ideas, however, are impotent unless they are implemented. Accordingly, the second goal was to develop the ability to initiate action and to mobilize efforts to carry out creative educational opportunities for children.

Understanding the resistances that might be encountered was critical. The new teachers would need to understand all the forces set in motion when one tries to alter the status quo: parents who consider themselves experts; teachers who regard suggestions for change as an implied criticism of their past efforts; school boards and administrators who see changes as bringing unpredictable consequences that make them vulnerable to censure; and taxpayers who measure all change with an economic yardstick.

The program also sought to prepare teachers who had an extensive theoretical background in the social sciences and firsthand knowledge of the poor and of ethnic group cultures. The reasoning here was that with this background, the teacher leaders would be able to begin to understand the causes and effects of poverty and the potential of educational institutions for individual development and for social change. Specifically, students were expected to understand the effects of poverty upon a family's life, to understand the problems of the poor as seen by the poor themselves, to be aware of the pressures placed upon poor families, and to identify factors in the home that contribute to learning or nonlearning in the school. In addition, knowledge about other cultures would facilitate building upon rather than ignoring the cultures' contributions when developing programs for the schools.

That participants have knowledge of the forces governing human behavior was also considered desirable. Without such knowledge, they would not be able to understand themselves and their motivations for actions, much less be able to work productively with others.

The Teacher Leader Program was also targeted at fostering in its participants positive and optimistic attitudes toward the possibility of improving learning opportunities for the poor. No amount of knowledge would suffice without an accompanying attitude of hope and a conviction that change is possible.

Another assumption of the project was that a program to prepare a small group of teachers must rely upon a multiplier effect to make an impact.

The program was thus designed to prepare teachers who would be able to assume more and more leadership in the education profession—that is, teachers who could generate interest and involvement among those whose influence might improve the effectiveness of persons whose lives touch children. Since alternative patterns of organization were considered necessary if schools are to serve their clients effectively, another program goal was for participants to learn skills that would help them allocate staff, time, space, and other resources in new and better ways.

Finally, the program was directed at developing in prospective teachers a repertoire of instructional modes as well as the knowledge to apply them appropriately. In order to do so, participants had to learn to assess children's needs and learning styles and then vary their strategies in response to differing situations.

To accomplish the objectives of the program, means were provided for its participants to learn to teach while avoiding the institutionalized forces that inhibit flexibility and limit the ability to act upon as well as to see alternatives. So that the future teachers might become aware of the purposes and potential of the schools, *they* were expected to establish and develop microcosmic educational enterprises. To meet this expectation, they had to find answers to such questions as the following:

What do the people in the community want a school to provide?

What should be taught and what is the best way to teach it?

Toward whom should the school be targeted?

How should children or youth be organized for the most effective teaching and learning?

How shall the enterprise be supported?

How can support be elicited from various constituencies?

Where shall the school be located?

How can the project be efficiently staffed?

In seeking answers to these questions, the participants discovered that there were fundamental questions about the schooling process and its purpose that must be addressed first. Ultimately, in *each* minischool, creative answers to these questions and solutions to problems had to be found.

A safeguard was guilt into the plan since the minischools were endowed with a stipulated lifespan. A maximum longevity of six weeks insured that unfortunate decisions would not be memorialized in enduring failure. It also protected all concerned against the unwelcome byproducts of success. A project would not get out of hand and become too big for the schoolmakers to handle. There would be no drive to perpetuate an enterprise for its own sake and have it thus become yet another institution that has lost its responsiveness to the needs of the people for whom it was designed.

During the academic year, the graduate students acquired many abilities that would enable them to run their little schools in the summer time. A year-long program provided the continual study and preparation needed for the schoolmaking projects.

The minischool programs would require participants to apply selectively the theoretical and practical understandings gained in their academic seminars and field experiences. Their responding honestly and empathically in personal contacts with community people would be necessary if they were to develop purposeful relationships directed toward making an impact on the lives of children. They would need sensitivity and understanding if they were to create programs that would attract, interest, and satisfy children who considered schools and schooling as unpleasant and unreal. The participants would have to recognize and utilize their own strengths and resources in directing staff and curriculum development toward overcoming learning problems.

In addition, the schoolmakers would have to recognize, to accept, and to understand the modes of communication employed by the poor: the use of nonverbal or, possibly, "nonstandard" or different verbal idioms. They needed to become familiar with the experiential contexts in which language and concepts are embedded. They would have to be able to function in diverse situations without appearing judgmental or patronizing.

The selection of children to participate in the minischools and the physical sites for the projects would require justification, with explicit rationales to be developed through the year's research, reading, and experience. Recruitment of these children (and their parents) would require many talents, as would the development and training of participating staff and the implementation of unique, innovative, meaningful programs.

Diagnostic skills would be of the highest importance if schoolmaker participants were to identify the needs of the community, both generally and with specific reference to the values and problems of particular subcultures, groups, families, and individual persons. Further, participants would have to observe and critically evaluate structures, programs, and activities the schools in the community were currently employing. By building on these, or compensating for them, the schoolmakers' task would be to plan curriculum, to select and develop materials, and to use instructional skills, maneuvers, and strategies to achieve their goals.

The program was created to foster informed, sensitive decision making in areas that would positively affect educational outcomes for the powerless. The minischool concept was central to the design of the program. This concept rested upon the assumption that people must have opportunity to engage in the behaviors they are expected to learn. Through such engagement they may develop power—confidence and competence—in the performance of those behaviors. Because the schoolmaking activities would require flexible selection from among a broad repertoire of behaviors by the future teachers, the mini-school enterprises promised their students benefits that would extend beyond the immediate impact of one summer.

3 The Schoolmakers

Fifteen candidates eager to become teachers and change agents were chosen to develop minischools. The Teacher Leader Program was designed to provide for all participants a broad array of experiences with children of different ages and with children in various ethnic communities. However, many among the fifteen persons selected for participation in the program were clearly attracted to children in specific age groups and to those of particular ethnic background. By and large, the interests of the schoolmakers might have been predicted by their backgrounds and prior experiences. These interests were expressed in the personal statements that accompanied their applications for admission to the program. Shared commitments drew most participants into close working relationships, which resulted in four cooperative minischool endeavors, while two participants chose to work on their own.

From the beginning, three participants—Stuart, Ben, and Clive, who had all majored in sociology—revealed special concern for the problems of teen-aged youth. They established their minischool, the Urban Studies Workshop, with a particular purpose in mind. They wanted to help a multi-ethnic group of adolescents develop understanding of themselves as interdependent social beings.

Although the three had all grown up in Los Angeles, their experiences were confined to different subcultural enclaves, and their shared concerns would not have brought them together had they not participated in the Teacher Leader Program. As a team, they targeted their minischool toward helping young people cope with the problems of urban living.

Ben, a tall, intense young man from a middle-class Jewish family, approached all problems with a baffling combination of cynicism and hope. He had attended a small college not far from the central city. His interest in urban educational problems came into focus during a project that brought college students together with youngsters from a dilapidated housing development in Los Angeles. Ben felt that he had gained more than he contributed in the course of this involvement: "It has made me well aware of the gross inadequacies of their environment, of the lack of facilities that are provided for them in their development."

Additionally, Ben worked as a noon recreation director at a school where the children were predominantly Mexican-American. Through his experiences Ben became convinced that social change must come about through education. Ben communicated this conviction when he applied to the Teacher Leader

17

Program and indicated that his eagerness to be part of the change process caused him to seek professional preparation:

My participation in . . . many satisfying experiences, and many difficult, unpleasant ones . . . has illuminated my future path, making clear to me that I want to enter the field of education. I want very much . . . to discover better and more effective methods in teaching, and I want to utilize and apply these methods where they are most needed in the poverty pockets of our communities. Some think education is a product of social change. I feel education is an important part of its cause. I want to be part of that cause and change.

Stuart, too, expressed a profound conviction that a system of education is pervasive in its influence. His experiences as a Peace Corps volunteer in Nigeria persuaded "Stu" that inadequate education not only deprives individual students but has wide-ranging results detrimental to their society:

It was in Nigeria that I saw firsthand what a lack of an education can mean to a young boy or girl who for one reason or another was not able to get the chance to enter a school. Not only was it a tremendous waste in talent, but it was an undeserved burden on the life of an individual who in many cases was extremely gifted intellectually and had the ability to do well in school but lacked the funds necessary to pay the fees.

Seeing the kind of education received in Nigeria by those who could afford the expense of schooling, Stu commented dismally:

In most cases it was poor in quality in that it lacked a creative approach to the learning process and stressed in its place rote learning. Students who graduated from the secondary schools, though knowing many facts, lacked the ability to solve problems and figure out solutions through an inquisitive reasoning process. The cumulative effect this had on the country as a whole was immeasurable.

Stu was a product of a Russian family, and his background was in sharp contrast to that of his teammates. Unlike Ben, Stu seemed to be always joking and never to take matters seriously. However, in his written assessment of the source of problems confronting socially disadvantaged groups, Stu quite soberly indicted the education they had received. As he wrote, he drew continuously upon his African experience:

I believe that a valid comparison can be made between the poor and the minority groups in this country with those peoples living in underdeveloped areas of the world. Lack of a sound educational experience in the past has provided much of the basis for the current social and economic deprivation now existing within their communities.

Stu commented that gains in alleviating deprivation must start with the educational process. He felt that he could contribute "to the national and international effort of raising the standard of living among peoples now living at a subsistence level." He was torn between his desire to teach at the secondary school level in one of this country's ghetto areas and his commitment to the Nigerians, which would mean returning to Africa. Either way, Stu was eager to get started: "I would like to do this now but realize that even with the best of intentions I must have more training and knowledge within the field of education to be able to do any kind of an effective job."

Although Clive's home was in the same general area as those of his team-mates, he was unlike Stu and Ben since he knew from personal experience the problems of membership in a visible minority group. A taciturn, athletic young man of commanding proportion, Clive's physical presence seemed to dominate any group. His ambition was to return to the communities from which he had come in order to make them better:

Having lived in the Mexican-American and black communities of Los Angeles for a total of fifteen years, I feel an obligation, as a humanitarian and concerned black man, to return to these communities and aid as many youths as possible in a teaching capacity. Having received my high school education in a ghetto school, I know many of the problems faced by these youths. It has been my life-long goal to do all I can to ameliorate as many of these problems as possible. I feel that this program for those interested in teaching the "disadvantaged" is an opportunity for me to move in this direction.

At the small southwestern college where Clive had recently earned a bachelor of arts degree, he found intellectual pursuits congenial to his interest in philosophical issues. He adapted easily to college life. Seeking to encourage his "brothers" to involve themselves with issues and ideas also, Clive worked as a tutor and counselor in Upward Bound. In this program he concentrated on helping minority youngsters of high school age prepare for higher education. He looked toward a teaching career to give permanence to his commitment. Along with Ben and Stu, Clive saw in their minischool, the Urban Studies Workshop, a way of sharpening the tools by which this commitment might be met.

La Escuelita, the summer manifestation of another minischool team's particular commitment, was oriented toward the specialized needs of young Mexican-American children. Flora, Maria, and Victor, the Teacher Leader Program's three Chicanos and its only married participants, accepted two of their "Anglo" fellows into the planning group for La Escuelita. They recognized in the two Anglo women participants special qualities that would complement their own commitment without jeopardizing the ethnocentric values that propelled it. When one of these two left the program at the beginning of the summer in order to teach in a remote Mexican village, the other, Sylvia, continued to work with the three Chicanos and added her particular insights to their determination and dedication.

Sylvia was an amputee who was still adjusting to her loss the previous spring. In addition to problems associated with physical disability, Sylvia had experienced poverty and the status of membership in a Portugese minority community within an agricultural area. As a result, she had a finely tuned sensitivity to the plight of children who, because of one kind of handicap or another, must battle against large odds. She involved herself with many such children during a work-study program in college and also as a volunteer. Sylvia had been an elementary school teaching assistant; she had worked as a counselor and tutor in Upward Bound.

Although occasionally silent and withdrawn, Sylvia harbored strong feelings about the necessity of educational change. When aroused to this topic, her eyes thundered darkly and her hands moved rapidly to cut through a torrent of words. On such occasions Sylvia revealed not only an amazing personal vitality, but also the strength of the convictions that drove her. She expressed these convictions less dynamically in the written statement that accompanied her application:

Many education systems which have been designed to promote academic success among "deprived" children have placed their emphasis on providing the kinds of stimulation and opportunities found in middle class environments. In order to attain the benefits of this kind of stimulation, the child must learn to adopt the values of the middle class because he must achieve in a school system structured on these values. It is the exceptional child who can learn to discriminate between the values necessary for success in school and those necessary for survival in his environment . . . I believe education must teach a child to understand and effectively cope with his environment without depriving him of his means of survival.

Sylvia concluded her personal statement on a prayerful note: "I hope to continue my education specializing in the remediation of learning disabilities and in counseling." She wanted "to become an instrument of change within an educational system that has failed so many children."

Maria had experienced the problems about which Sylvia expressed concern; she knew the difficulty of survival in an environment characterized by cultural confict. The second eldest of eleven children, "Mia" had personally faced the problem of school expectations that confront Spanish-speaking children having substantial home responsibilities:

My early educational experiences have made an immeasurable impression on my life and world view. My elementary school years were torturous. I hated school because I was never able to succeed, regardless of how hard I tried. I was always behind and in the "slow group." I knew that I was considered stupid and a slow learner. I suppose the problem was that I didn't speak any

English when I entered school. This problem was compounded by the fact that my home environment was terriby noisy and crowded, making studying extremely difficult. As a child and teenager I had many child-care and household responsibilities so extensive that I had a limited childhood. I can remember feeling miserable, sometimes at the point of tears, because my teachers and classmates ridiculed me for being different. I cannot forget how inadequate and inferior I felt.

Mia explained that gradually and with much effort her grades began to improve in junior high school. Despite early and some continuing handicaps, she was an award-winning high school student who earned further distinction at the community college serving the area in which she lived. There she established a tutorial society for Mexican-American high school students in difficulty, and she served at a community center in an alienated neighborhood.

Continuing her work-study at a small liberal arts college, Mia received a B.A. in sociology just prior to applying for admission to the program. She had played an active role in a politically oriented Chicano student group and in the development of the Mexican-American Studies Center. However, unlike more overtly rebellious students, Maria worked through the established system in seeking solutions to the educational problems posed by language and value conflicts. While still an undergraduate, she studied the possibility of establishing a bilingual elementary school. In her statement of purpose Mia declared profound interest in a teacher education program that encouraged the creation of innovative curricula for culturally different students. She believed that such students pose to education "its most formidable challenge of the present decade," and she denounced traditional approaches, which she regarded as exacerbating a serious social problem:

Bilingual, bicultural children have suffered dearly because the educational system has been oblivious to the child's needs and environment. Bilingual children have been unduly penalized by the education process for coming to school with a different learning structure, personality and value system. Traditional educational institutions are capable of doing nothing more than stifling, ultimately killing a child's desire to question, explore, create, and learn.

Like Maria, Victor (who demanded that his name be pronounced *Victór*) also stated that he had "suffered the trauma" of a non English–speaking child in a school environment indifferent to his needs. The result was a single-minded concern with making the educational system relevant to the needs of his people:

My own personal experience as a Chicano plus having tutored and worked in elementary schools in the barrios and other poverty areas make the needs appear more pressing. The home environment and elementary school experience are the foundation upon which all is built. In order to preserve the values of the Chicano culture and to keep the elementary school experience from clashing with these values, thus causing the majority of Chicanos to drop out, I feel the implementation of bilingual-bicultural education is a step towards solving the problem.

With the unexpected vacating of one fellowship soon after the program began, militant Victor had been selected by his peers for late entry into the program. He was chosen because of his devotion to his people that bordered on tortured obsession and because of his deep commitment to educational change. Among Victor's other qualifications was an ability to persevere, which had enabled him to return to his schooling following a tour with the armed services. With a wife and child to care for, he was determined enough to complete work toward a B.A. in Spanish and history at a California state college. Along with a degree, Victor also received a scholarship award for distinction in intergroup education and thus was able to continue his studies.

For Flora, who was older than the other participants, completing her undergraduate studies had not been easy either. With three of her four children in school, Flora returned, part-time, to her own education; after four years of study in various community colleges near her home, she completed requirements for an associate of arts degree with honors. She then went on to receive a baccalaureate in two years and finished this undergraduate work just in time to enter the program. Although her college involvement focused continuously on the social sciences, Flora increasingly directed its thrust toward the development of opportunity for those within the Mexican-American community. In her application, she stated: "I have been particularly interested in problems related to Mexican-American children and have done extensive research in this area." She explained that her work with these children took her into schools with a large Chicano enrollment. A member of the Mexican-American Political Association, Flora was concerned with providing college scholarships for Mexican-American students, and she worked tirelessly toward this end.

As a fourth generation Californian whose mother was Mexican-American, Flora was highly sensitive to the culture and traditions indigenous to the Southwest. She said she was looking forward to teaching in a situation in which such sensitivity was particularly needed. She saw La Escuelita as just such a situation and along with those sharing her special concerns, Flora welcomed the opportunity to develop the minischool.

In a sense, the Ramona Minischool was a test of hypotheses formulated during a year of academic study and of tentative exploration into school communities. Both Maxine and Helga who ran this program were blond, blue-eyed "Anglos" who, separately, had returned recently from Peace Corps service in underdeveloped regions. When applying to the program, Helga had just come back from a year of teaching Liberian youngsters in a tribal village—an experience that made her aware of the importance of communication to the educational process:

I was the first grade teacher for fifty Kru children whose ages ranged from six to seventeen years old. Half of the children were repeating first grade; the other half were coming from kindergarten. My main task was to teach them English; they didn't speak much English and I didn't speak much Kru. Consequently, we had communication problems.

In her letter requesting admission to the program, Helga had no difficulty communicating the sense of frustration she felt in trying to establish a good learning environment for children who had learned to respect only the authority of the switch. The fact that she survived the year and still wanted to teach indicated to the program's admissions committee something of the depth of her commitment and the sincerity of her words. She wrote:

I faced many problems which I tried to solve with my own ideas. I was in an isolated village, so books and advisors were not available to me. Before I go back into teaching I would like to get some answers, and if they aren't available, at least some suggestions from educators who share a similar view of education with me. . . . My experiences have led me to believe that the traditional type of American education is greatly lacking in fulfilling the goal of educating our children. In order to have a truly effective educational system, the parents, teachers, community and school officials must all work together. In Liberia, most of the parents have never attended school. Consequently they don't give active support to the school, the teachers, or their children.

Helga had not always been interested in becoming a teacher. As a biochemistry major, her first three years at a north-central university were spent in laboratories. Then in her senior year, Helga had switched to a political science major. She indicated that she wanted "to find out about human beings and what they were doing," not more about their chemical composition. But making up the academic requirements to complete her new major in order to graduate in 1968 had left her little time for human involvement. So Helga volunteered for the Peace Corps and went to live among the Kru people. She chose to involve herself with the children's introductory school experiences because she wanted to give young Liberians a foundation based upon more than the routine memorization that characterized the educational methods used in their country:

Well, I found out that I love to work with children, and that I care about the type of education they receive. Especially since I feel that I was robbed as a child. I was taught to perform for the teacher and to always give the right answers (the ones the teacher wanted). I was always scared to speak out in class for fear that I might give a wrong answer (that I might displease the teacher). I had to be at the top of my class so that I would please my parents and my teacher. I really didn't care about what I was learning. I found that if I really got interested in something, I wouldn't have the time to study it because there were too many other assignments demanding my attention. I would like to have a classroom where this type of pressure is not placed on the child. If we can get innovative teaching in the classroom, we will have more responsible, interesting, creative, and innovative adults in the future. I guess that is the key reason why I'm choosing teaching for a career. When I think about the problems of the world, and especially the problems of America, I'm greatly distressed and saddened. My reaction is to either become a hermit or to do what I can to change American life. I've opted for doing what I can. What better way than to teach our children so that they can better cope with the problems of our human existence.

Through her experiences in Liberia, Helga became convinced that for such teaching to be effective schooling must not be separated from all other parts of children's lives:

The parents and the community environment are the major factors in determining how the child views his school and his teachers, and more important, in determining how the child approaches the whole process of finding out about the world. When there is no support from the community, or even worse, when there is negative influence, the educational process can not truly be successful. I want to be involved in a program that attempts to bring the teachers, parents, community, and school officials together in their efforts to change the present American educational system.

Helga saw the Teacher Leader Program as contributing to such efforts. She looked upon the opportunity to develop a minischool as a way of turning big ideas into that small reality necessary to every beginning. And sharing her enthusiasm for the opportunity presented by the schoolmaking project was Maxine, Helga's partner in the Ramona Minischool.

Maxine had found her Peace Corps experience so rewarding that she wanted to bring the joy of cross-cultural experience to others. She regarded such experience as essential to true progress in various walks of life. She observed: "In whatever role, we may begin the step toward understanding by being sensitive to different culture patterns." This participant was, herself, particularly sensitive to language differences and to the subtle variances in world view that such differences signaled.

Maxine had concentrated upon studies in Spanish at the Universidad de Mexico as well as the northwestern university where she took her degree. Subsequently, she not only gained wide experience with the language, but also learned Guarani during two years of volunteer work with the Peace Corps as a Home Extension Agent in Paraguay. There, she taught nutrition and health, worked with local 4-H clubs, and organized a local school for the Paraguayan Extension Service, a school in which club leaders studied all areas of home economics. Upon her return to the United States, Maxine became both a language and a technical instructor for the Peace Corps in a West Coast development and training center. That she found this work gratifying became apparent when she wrote:

Since I have enjoyed using my Spanish so very much, I would like to stay in the field—as a teacher at any level. . . . I hope to bring my experience in a Latin culture to any position or studies program I enter, always hoping that the Spanish idiom and culture play a large part.

Ambitious, certain of her goals, and constantly striving for perfection, Maxine wanted to be in the program because she saw it as an opportunity to further expand her ability to influence the direction of lives circumscribed by ethnocentrism and provincialism as well as by poverty. She felt that cross-cultural encounter could be an enriching experience for all involved. Together, Maxine and Helga sought solutions to problems created by limited alternatives being available to children, as well as by the limited security in which alternatives might be investigated. They tested and refined these solutions in the Ramona Minischool they created on the site of a housing project.

Some ten miles from Ramona, in another housing project, the members of yet another white Anglo team tested their ability to cross cultural boundaries and to meet people on their own ground. They set up the Las Palmas Minischool in the project's community house. In doing this, Boyd, Gail, and Tina attempted to answer some persistent and difficult questions.

The most theoretically oriented of the participants, Boyd raised the most abstract questions. Of Norwegian heritage, he was unpredictable and shifted between intellectual intensity, playfulness, and impenetrable silences. During the academic year of preparation for teaching, he posed searching and sometimes irritatingly unanswerable questions with regard to critical educational issues. When applying for admission to the program, Boyd gave warning of the challenge he would present. Drawing on his recent experiences, from which had arisen a persistent interest in the role of language as a determinant of behavior and personality, Boyd pondered such puzzlers as "What happens in a bilingual mind?" He wanted to understand the ways in which language and culture interact and to use such knowledge as a resource in the teaching and learning process. "What is learning?" he demanded. When there are competing explanations (biochemical, developmental, and others), how do you choose among them and make them "work for you?" Questions appearing in the personal statement accompanying Boyd's application demanded thoughtful consideration if establishment of a sound school program was to be achieved.

Many questions asked by Boyd were those all participants had to address during the year of preparation for schoolmaking:

Realistically, can the school function in any meaningful surrogate role as parents?

How can you compensate for children's stark environments?

What are ways to initially provide success for these kids and to sustain it?

What materials and methods work best for so-called disadvantaged kids?

Why a school with four walls?

Boyd felt that his experience qualified him to contribute to a program dedicated to helping resolve the issues implied in these questions. "The question of innovation and imagination are no longer issues for me," he said; "How you bring change becomes the issue."

Before his graduation from a north-central university in 1969, Boyd, a political science major, had spent six months in Costa Rica as a research assistant investigating agrarian reform. There he became fluent in Spanish and gained insight into peasant culture. These were extended during a month of living with a Mexican family in Coahuila.

After earning his degree, Boyd volunteered as a tutor in a federal program for Portuguese and Puerto Ricans in Boston. There, in an urban setting, he became involved in a bilingual program for out-of-school Spanish-speaking children. In that program, Boyd perceived a central problem to be the unresolved conflict between the dominant, urban, secular society and a first-generation immigrant group. He perceived that the newcomers were guided by a tradition-directed value system that elicited rigid, authoritarian views on education, discipline, and child growth. He saw the New England program as placing heavy emphasis upon the parent and community involvement of "an awakening minority." As a consequence of that experience, Boyd claimed profound awareness of "problems of the school and society that must always be confronted and acted on." He was eager to be a part of the action.

For Gail and Tina, painful questions arose in the context of the year's program that was preparatory to their minischool involvement. They became increasingly aware of the commitment to self-determination emerging within the black community with which they had become involved. They struggled with issues associated with their own roles in this process. Ultimately, they decided to join Boyd in planning and operating a minischool for a predominantly Mexican-American population in the public housing project known as "Las Palmas."

Tina's interest in working with young black children had been stimulated during her undergraduate days at the eastern college where she earned a degree in 1968. She had been involved in summer camps and in work with under-privileged city children. Following graduation, she was eager to develop the ability to work more effectively with children and did a semester of specialized work in teacher education at an East Coast college. Convinced that an effective school experience is critical to the child's future, Tina had worked with Head Start and had been a "master teacher" in a day care center run by the Office of Educational Opportunity. Still, she was dissatisfied with her own performance. When applying for admission to the program, she stated, "I was constantly aware that I was unprepared to do an effective job, however good my instincts might be."

The "instincts" of which Tina spoke seemed to have arisen from intense feelings about her own formative years spent in classrooms:

I found that I lived up to the expectations of those teachers who were interested in the students, who created a good feeling in the class, who encouraged that each child find her own way. Happy with my school life, I was able to deal confidently and constructively with other experiences. On the other hand, I can remember how easily I was discouraged from experimenting or doing more than they required with teachers who stressed factual learning, who insisted on one method of attacking problems, who brought a sense of competition and pressure to the class.

Tina expressed a need to gain experience with

. . . competent, thinking teachers, to discuss and evaluate with other teachers their problems and ways of dealing with them, to think more deeply about the kinds of experiences which are important to bring to a classroom, and generally to evolve a whole concept of what the school should be striving towards. I'm also interested in developing an approach which involves a great deal of music, dance, and improvisational drama. I feel that children respond easily to that approach because it offers an area in which children who are not ordinarily successful in the classroom may find competence, and because it is a good way for children to express their emotions constructively.

With a profound appreciation of the value to learners of the expressive arts, Tina was attracted to programs for young children. She not only found difficulty in compartmentalizing the learning process and the learner, but also in fragmenting herself:

It is important to me that I have work for which I am wholly responsible and which demands great energy and attention. Teaching is just the kind of experience where one both conceives of and implements a whole program.

Tina was especially interested in the Teacher Leader Program because of its emphasis on helping the child within his or her environment. In her personal statement that accompanied the application she sent from Africa, Tina explained her reason for this interest:

It was difficult to establish any communication with the parents in many of the programs in which I've been involved. For this reason, it was always difficult to get a good picture of the children and of the feelings and concepts they were bringing into school with them.

Unlike Tina, Gail already had some experience working among Chicanos. She was familiar with "the feelings and concepts" some of the children brought with them to Las Palmas. After a variety of summer work experiences during college years in New England, Gail, who had majored in music, joined VISTA. She worked with the high school youth of a Mexican-American community in the Rocky Mountain region. She assessed her facility with Spanish as "passable."

Honey-toned in appearance, Gail was described by one of her fellow participants as "a shaft of wheat." During her VISTA service, she lived quietly in a poverty area and counseled students with school attendance problems, some of whom were known to the courts:

At first the problems, such as dropout rates, reading problems, nonattenadance, and nonschool-community relations, seemed insoluble. Tutoring individual students was the only thing that proved at all successful, but even that included frustrating and baffling failures. It seems that there are always day-to-day traumas in the lives of the kids which affect very greatly their attitude in the classroom—traumas that a typical teacher never knows about and thus this teacher never really understands why the kid has "learning problems."

Concerned with enlarging and extending the benefits of the VISTA-sponsored tutorial program, Gail set up a youth-tutoring-youth project that brought high school and elementary students together to the advantage of each group. In assessing her experience in VISTA, this applicant was enthusiastic about the potential for change inherent in programs that have flexibility as their hallmark:

It seems to me that in disadvantaged areas, educational methods are just not working, partly because they were not set up with these areas in mind. The street academy approach is probably the most successful thing that I have seen in the area of education, but it needs to be expanded. Education could be a vehicle for the solution of many related problems in poverty areas if it would only be allowed to be flexible enough to become that vehicle.

The opportunity to develop a minischool Gail viewed as "exciting."

The obsessive commitment to self-determination among blacks had caused Tina and Gail to test their ability to teach "culturally different" children within a nonblack ethnic enclave, and this commitment was what impelled Cal. He detached himself from the group and affiliated his minischool with the Black School, a community-supported school run for and by blacks. Because he had attended schools and colleges in a range of social circumstances and environments, Cal felt qualified to judge the relevance of current educational practices to his people, and he was committed to increasing it:

I grew up in Virginia where I attended a segregated school for five years. Since then I have had the opportunity to attend schools and colleges in what I believe to be a good cross-section of this country's school system (the urban ghetto— Watts—the rural midwest, and the white middle-class suburb). In each instance, I have viewed the curriculum through the eyes of a black student. All proved to be irrelevant to the black student. . . . It is my goal to help develop and improve the relevance of education to the student. Being black, I believe that I can aid in the educational development of black students.

Throughout his college days Cal had worked to improve the quality of "the black experience." He had done this in a number of ways: as president of an NAACP youth chapter; as a member of the Human Relations Council in each of three communities in which he had lived and studied; as a volunteer music teacher (clarinet, flute, and saxophone) to neighborhood children; as cofounder and director of a nonprofit music talent workshop; as athletic director at a Title I elementary school; and as president of his college's Black Student Union and editor of its paper. He was an athlete, as well as perennial worker at part-time jobs (including school noon aide). Not surprisingly, Cal had to scurry in order to complete his degree requirements in sociology in time for admission to the program. Within the program he said he hoped to "be a part of a group that will plan to make education not only relevant to the minority student but to all students." And in his statement to the program's admissions committee, there was only a hint of the conflicts Cal was experiencing:

It is hard to impart sincerity. To say that I love my people seems simpleton or as though I were a charlatan. I confess to harboring middle-class values; however, the empathy for my people pushes them aside.

Black also, Winifred most recently had directed a Teen-Post that was located at a church site in an urban setting. Through this experience she became aware that little black children in the neighborhood had serious needs that were not being met with any organized summer program. Despite a daily forty-mile round trip that resulted in her "going-it-alone" without peer support, "Freddi" dedicated herself to meeting the needs of these children by establishing the Live Oak Minischool.

To Freddi meeting the needs of children meant "teaching." In her personal statement Freddi underscored her aspirations with regard to a master's degree and a teaching credential:

My experience in tutoring elementary school children, conducting recreation programs, and working as a camp counselor to help supplement the regular school program has convinced me that my long desire to become a teacher should be fulfilled.

Freddi was quick to point out, however, that she did not regard academics alone to be sufficient preparation:

I do not believe that getting a degree, per se, will equip me to teach. My objectives are to gain enough insight to apply the principles learned during my studies and learning to help motivate, promote and encourage learning, to provide a myriad of opportunities for learning skills, and to provide a step process of preparing young people for future education so that someday they may take their places as responsible citizens in their community and society at large.

Freddi came to the program with a B.A. in sociology from a large southwestern college, and she brought with her considerable experience in people-to-people activities. A frequent recipient of scholarships and awards of recognition, she spent three months as a Sargent Shriver scholar in Bogotá, Colombia where she learned to communicate in Spanish. She served a year as acting director of a community center in a low-income area at the hub of an agricultural-industrial region. In addition, Freddi spent two summers as a volunteer with a program serving migrants. The selection committee was inclined to agree with her assessment when she stated: "I strongly feel that I have a lot to contribute to the field of Elementary Education." And there was similar concurrence that the broader purposes that Freddi expressed also represented an aspiration of the Teacher Leader Program:

I feel that what I will learn should benefit not only me, but should also be a means of exposing a larger American Public to the value of Education for better person-to-person, person-to-society, and person-to-community relations.

The six minischools, then, were developed and run by fourteen participants—three Mexican-Americans, three Afro-Americans, and the rest "Anglo"-Americans. Among the fourteen, two—Freddi and Cal—were "independents." One minischool was operated by two of the women participants, two minischools were developed by trios (one all male and one mixed), and there was one mixed foursome. Only two of the program participants were known to each other before the group came together in September of 1970.

The schoolmakers had been selected from 130 applicants during the preceding spring. At that time much attention was given to the choice of raw material. What qualities should be sought when choosing people for participation in such a project? To answer this question a committee was established to view the matter of participant selection from a variety of perspectives. The members were students, practicing teachers, faculty members, administrators, a psychiatrist, and representatives of black and Chicano communities.

The committee considered the children who were to be the ultimate beneficiaries of the program. Its members assumed that effective education for these children would require innovative solutions to educational problems and that the attributes characterizing a group of innovators might be identified.

From their discussions, two preeminent criteria for participation in the program surfaced: Those selected must show genuine interest in working with the young; in addition, they must have an authentic concern for the problems of persons caught in the web of poverty. Interest in children could be demonstrated through a record of voluntary involvement with projects and organizations associated with children or youth; concern for the plight of the poor, if not growing out of life experience, could be demonstrated through a record of personal engagement in seeking solutions to social problems.

Since work with people requires the ability to communicate with them in their own idiom, the committee looked for evidence that applicants were capable of learning to do so. The committee members viewed the ability to speak a second language as one indication of this capability, and facility in speaking the Spanish language was regarded even more positively because of the program's location in the Southwest.

The admissions committee was aware of the program's emphasis on problem solving and decided that the persons selected must show that they were challenged by situations for which no easy answers might be found. Applicants' records were studied for evidence that confronting problems was regarded as enjoyable and exciting. The participants definitely had to be risktakers since innovations are never covered by insurance of success. However, they had to have the intelligence to calculate realistically the risks involved, as well as the ability to optimize the growth of children under conditions less than optimal.

Inasmuch as working toward the program's goals would require collaborative efforts, participants were sought who would contribute complementary dimensions of understanding and experience. Applications were examined for evidence that the candidates were not only intelligent, with positive self-concepts, but that they enjoyed working with others and had demonstrated initiative, creativity, and leadership in their past endeavors. Although regular university admission requirements were considered, heaviest emphasis in selecting participants was placed upon evidence of academic *potential,* plus a *commitment* to teaching and to improving social conditions, as these were indicated in letters of recommendation and in applicants' personal statements.

The applicants' personal statements figured prominently in the selection process for two reasons. First, because of time and distance, no program of interviewing candidates was undertaken. Second, since emphasis was placed upon the importance of commitment and of communication skills, the selection committee took a hard look at that portion of the application in which commitment was most personally communicated. Committee members considered not only the intensity of commitment shown, but also the way in which it was manifested through action.

Of the group selected by the committee, fifteen participants went through the academic year together; one left the program at the beginning of the summer in order to teach children in a Mexican community where she had previously lived. The fourteen who remained—six men and eight women—established their educational programs in low-income communities in the summer of 1971. These were the fourteen program participants described earlier in this chapter. These were the participants who planned and implemented the six minischool programs that will be described in later chapters. These were the schoolmakers.

4   Getting Ready

The circular that announced the Teacher Leader Program was distributed nationwide. It solicited applications for admission during the spring of 1970. It featured the opportunity for schoolmaking, which was unique to the program. However, it did not specify the place of schoolmaking in relation to the total program; it did not explain that schoolmaking was a culminating and not an introductory experience.

The fifteen applicants who were selected for participation in the program were disappointed when they first came together. They found that a year-long program stood between them and the minischool adventure that had lured them to apply. Their disillusionment served as an immediate and common bond. They began the program with a generalized sense of dissatisfaction. Both their words and their actions suggested that the intellectual activities that had been planned for them were unnecessary. Academics could do little to enhance the spontaneous drive with which they entered the program. Apparently, the delay of even a week, much less a year, before they could put their minischools into operation was regarded by most as a waste of time and talent. The attributes that figured in the participants' selection—commitment, action orientation, enthusiasm, independence—meant that they were impatient with theory. The group's eagerness to acquire and to *use* specific teaching skills made the first-year curriculum a product of considerable negotiation. In this chapter, the preplanned program is described along with the participants' influence upon it.

The program's planners and faculty came to the first year with a particular orientation. They felt that there was much in the literature of many disciplines that would help the participants get ready for their schoolmaking endeavors. They wanted to help participants make rational decisions in order to maximize their chance of success in developing their minischools. There were strategies that could prove useful. The group also needed to examine attitudes about themselves and the learning process. Thus, the program planners felt that a period of preparation and planning was imperative. For this reason, a detailed program had been planned prior to the preterns' arrival (Figure 4-1). The planners realized, however, that what finally evolved would be a function of participant planning, as well as the ideas, needs, and personalities of the people for whom the program was intended.

Fortunately the program had been structured to give flexibility to both participants and staff. Designed for responsiveness to idiosyncratic, as well as broad needs and interests, it yielded to the overt and covert pressures brought

33

34

Program Components	Sept	Oct	Nov	Dec	Jan	Feb	Mar	Apr	May	June	July	Aug
		Fall Semester					Spring Semester				Summer	

Academic Work

Elective
Curriculum Study
Small Group Processes

Elective
Instructional Models
Organizational Change

Curriculum Studies

Minischools

Field Work*

1 2 3 4 5 6

7

8

Learning Community

Options Limited

Many Options

*Suggested Field Work Sequence:
1. Urban study trips.
2. Exploration in local school communities.
3. Identification of a child to tutor; community study from perspective of the home.
4. Observation-participation in the child's school and classroom.
5. Refocusing.
6. Refocusing and further classroom experience.
7. The Practicum: intensive in-classroom experience.
8. Wide-ranging exploration in preparation for minischools.

The First Year of the Two-Year Program to Develop Teacher Leaders Specializing in the Problems of the Disadvantaged

September 21, 1970 — August 8, 1971

Figure 4-1. The Planned Program.

to bear upon it. The participants were a significant influence upon the directions they each would take, not only because of the program's malleability, but also because their selection was predicated upon their potential for impact upon established institutions.

The criteria by which these young people had been selected militated against their docilely submitting themselves to a prestructured curriculum, although such a response would have made the staff's tasks easier. The commitment to institutional change that moved the participants to apply for admission to the program compelled them to challenge the program's design and to resist institutionalization of their activities in a monolithic structure. One of the participants, commenting on the group's counterdependent nature, wrote: "Anyone looking for the makings of a revolutionary army probably could not find a better lot of individuals to enlist."

The teacher preparation program's design rested upon several assumptions. These assumptions provided the program with the flexibility and resilience that allowed it to evolve. First was the tenet that theoretical and experimental learning should be dynamically interrelated. Second was the assumption that differences in students should be encouraged, for educators have found no one best way to learn and therefore no one best way to teach. Diversity of past experience among learners suggested a need for diversity among environments if there was to be an ideal relationship—an appropriate match—between the emotional, intellectual, and social states of the learner and those experiences by which growth becomes optimally extended. There was the expectation that every learner selects from a given learning experience what is personally most meaningful to him, and, therefore, the same outcomes cannot be expected from all students as a result of similar experiences.

Additionally, the planners assumed that since learning is an active and not a passive process, students must become involved in what they learn. They believed that effective learner activity occurs in a climate of emotional safety where the learner may risk making a "mistake" and that exploratory activity is fruitful even though it has neither immediate nor obvious "payoff." For the learner's capacities to be extended through exploration would require the support of a cooperative environment—that is, one in which people and institutions coexist in an atmosphere of open, free communication. Commitment to these ideas about learning were believed to apply at any level from preschool to postgraduate. The process of graduate education would be, therefore, an important element in its content. Such process-content suggests that the way people are taught will ultimately determine how they will teach.

The negotiation and planning that took place allowed all involved to agree upon certain objectives to be accomplished during the first year. However, realistically, the penchant for action made commitment to reflective learning on the part of the potential teacher leaders more tentative than it was on the part of the faculty. Since the preterns' overwhelming objective was to prepare themselves to work effectively with the poor (and in many cases culturally different), the many strands of the program centered about the key concept of "poverty," its causes, its nature, and its effects.

Because the participants came to the program with different backgrounds, some had to increase their firsthand knowledge of the poor and others had to sort out their feelings and reflect upon their own past experiences. In the end they would all have to understand both intellectually and empathically the effects of poverty upon a family's life, understand the problems of the poor as seen by the poor themselves, be aware of the pressures placed upon poor families, and identify factors in the home and in a child's total life space that contribute to his learning or not learning. Without this knowledge and insight the new teachers could not effectively build community learning centers attuned to the desires, needs, and expectations of children and their families.

Another focal point about which the curriculum was designed was based upon an understanding of the importance of communicating well in all types of situations. To marshal commitment toward a goal, to give or receive information, or to establish *esprit* and *camaraderie,* people must become aware of their impact upon others. Skill is especially needed when interacting persons have not grown up with the same experiences or language heritage. Knowledge of the communication process, the role of verbal and nonverbal media, and an understanding of one's own feelings are all necessary for honest and open communication. Experiences, classes, and readings during the year attempted to build expertise and skill in this area.

If the participants in the program were to make a difference in the quality of the life of the poor, they had to believe that they were capable of making changes. Confidence supported by positive and optimistic attitudes was necessary. The possibility of helping others had to seem realistic. Through an acquaintance with many strategies for teaching and the opportunity to try them out, the students would be able to develop and to feel their power as teachers, and hopefully, experiences with many contexts in which learning was possible would help them to develop positive, constructive, and realistic expectations.

Children who are poor have special needs—often basic needs related to physical survival, such as for services that insure meeting health, safety, and nutritional requirements. Parents of adequate means can take advantage of resources available in the community and are able to solve problems that are insurmountable to poor, illiterate, or overworked parents. By increasing their knowledge about resources for helping the children, new teachers would gain influence over the lives of those children. The needed resources might lie outside the school or might be available through an adaptive, innovative curriculum within the classroom. Wherever such resources were, finding and putting them to use would be incumbent upon the intern teachers.

To be effective, the planning process should involve the persons affected by it. The program was intended, therefore, to provide the graduate students with the skill to involve the poor in changing their own situations—that is, in mutual goal setting in the development of programs to achieve the desired objectives. If new ideas and strategies were to be initiated and implemented, participants needed to strengthen their ability to work cooperatively not only with those they wished to help, but also with school personnel, social and political groups and agencies, and with colleagues. The preservice year's program was designed to achieve these objectives. The people responsible for implementing the graduate curriculum worked to see that academic considerations in the seminars and practical considerations in the participants' field experiences followed parallel paths and that there were mechanisms for linking these.

The academic component of the program was dissimilar to conventional teacher preparation programs in an important way: its interdisciplinary thrust. Through study in the social and behavioral sciences the students were able to gain a broad theoretical perspective about problems associated with cultural differences and the effects of poverty upon a society.

Two courses, one in social psychology and the other in anthropology, were taken by the group as a whole. The first, which addressed "small group processes," was selected because it was felt that all of the potential leaders would at some time have to make use of skills and theoretical knowledge regarding how groups are formed and how they function. However, when the instructor met with and began to understand the group, he recognized that the curriculum he had originally regarded as appropriate was in fact unsuitable:

The intention of my course was to get the interns acquainted with the principles of group dynamics and I had planned that it be relatively unstructured, using the behavior of the group to help it to look at how groups work.

The course, which had not been planned to meet at regular intervals, began with a weekend session:

To begin with I had planned an intensive weekend session, but it was difficult to get going. Much of the energy that first weekend was devoted to resistance.

Because of the group's hostility to becoming involved in "sensitivity training," the instructor decided to alter his teaching strategy and revert to more traditional methods:

Adapting to the situation, in subsequent sessions I turned to a teaching-lecturing format and provided the students with simulations and relatively structured laboratory "games" such as NASA's "Man on the Moon." Participation became enthusiastic and I think the natural leaders in the group emerged.

That the seminar began painfully and established an abrasive climate was probably due to participant resistance arising from two sources. The first was the hostility of the blacks and Chicanos, who thought the study of group dynamics a "white missionary device"; the second was because the course had been "required":

In the end the experience was really worthwhile. We ended on a relatively good note, although I never had an experience with a group in which I felt so much hostility toward myself by a small minority. I don't think the course was the flop I thought it was at the time. I had been hoping for a really good experience, but the group reading of the experience as "mandatory" helped those who were resistant to turn out really resistant. I was reminded of working with Peace Corps volunteers. You are really trying to appeal to people who think of themselves as independent. When people get the idea "El Gringo has come to save you" they dig in their heels.

From the experience, the participants learned about themselves and about people's responses to mandated programs. Although counseling the preterns was unplanned, the instructor became an informal consultant to many of them during the whole program:

They came and told me things that had happened to them. They would appear singly or in two's and three's at unexpected times. I saw at least half of them for the rest of the year, anyway. I didn't anticipate that. The fact that they were all leaders made it difficult for them to sit down in a group and work together. My final feeling was very positive.

A second mandated course dealt with communication and cultural dissonance. Its original objective was to analyze the nature of cultural differences and their effects upon the communication process across societies. A substantial part of the course had been prepared in advance of the first session. Information from distant cultures and principles of broad general applicability had been collected to be used by the professor to introduce the study of cultural distinctiveness.

The instructor's intention had been to go from broad abstract concepts to applications in solving concrete problems. Again the will of the group made modification necessary:

During this first session the planned structure became obviously inoperable. So motivated was the majority of the students to enter directly the hard facts of ethnicity and educational opportunity that such an orientation of subject matter or a detached attitude toward it would not work.

The professor therefore realized that instruction had to begin with the interests of these highly committed students—that is, with the problems of the poor in *this* country:

The large facts of anthropological research concerned with man in general and in distant societies, had to be accommodated to the immediate interests of the students. Thus the course, its purposes, content, and methods were open to continual negotiation.

Small work groups evolved. Each dealt with content of the group's selection and used the instructor as a resource person who was able to contribute anthropological principles and facts as well as methods of inquiry. The students' orientation forced immediate highlighting of actual social problems.

Other courses were taken individually or in small groups after the participants considered elective courses available to them.[a] One participant said he felt "like a little boy with a big jar of candy" from which he had to make a choice. The first semester, two participants opted to work in the area of Mexican-American studies. Twelve (including two Chicanos) chose courses in black studies. Two blacks and seven Anglos enrolled in one course that seemed of almost universal interest: Social Psychological Aspects of Black Identity. It was offered by a black psychologist.

The students electing Mexican-American studies expressed enthuasism for their work and made frequent conversational reference to their readings and the understandings they were developing. The Chicanos in black studies maintained contact with the Mexican-American Studies Center and continued to work independently in this area. The preterns in the black psychology course found it emotionally demanding; the whites, especially, gained unexpected if painful insights into their own behavior as well as the behavior of black children.

In the second semester three interns chose black studies courses; four opted for Chicano studies. Five of the students, feeling the need for increased professional knowledge, chose instead to enroll in an education course that addressed problems in reading. One became interested in a course in linguistics.

A link between the theoretical knowledge the preterns were gaining in their academic seminars and the application of that knowledge to practical considerations in the communities of the poor was provided in the form of a seminar in education in which all participants were involved. It dealt with two

---

[a]Representative courses were: Blacks and the Communication Media; The Black American in the 20th Century; Economics of Pocket Development: The Ghetto; Race Consciousness, Mental Health and Personality Development; Chicano Politics: The Search for Community Power; Sociology of the Mexican American; Race Relations; Social Stratification; Comparative Urbanization; Power and Change; The Social Psychological Aspects of Black Identity.

aspects of schooling. The first was concerned with the problem of developing a conceptual framework around which new, innovative, and relevant programs congruent with the children's needs and interests could be designed. The second was targeted at helping the future teachers acquire a repertoire of teaching strategies that could be used to help youngsters learn.

The major objective of the seminar was to increase the options open to a dynamic teacher in any given situation. The seminar was not intended to prescribe or recommend patterns of teaching behavior—a tactic often employed by educators in other settings—but rather, students were encouraged to make rational choices about effective means to achieve agreed-upon ends and to deal intelligently and resourcefully with the reality of given situations. In this seminar, the faculty strived to make the future teachers aware of the problems that exist and help them to generate as many solutions as possible. Rather than accepting a one best method, the students were encouraged to use the knowledge they had in order to select for implementation the alternative that seemed most appropriate in a given situation. If a tentative solution proved ineffective, it would provide additional data for the selection of another alternative.

The participants in the seminar were asked to address themselves to three questions: "What's happening?" "What should be happening?" "How can we make it happen?" As expected, all the participants felt they knew a great deal about the first question, either because of firsthand experience or because they were avid readers of educational critics such as Kohl, Kozol, and Leonard. Commenting on one of the field trips undertaken to gather data about "What's happening?" Cal wrote in his journal:

These two days have had a nostalgic effect on me. I felt much as a bandit. As in a freak show, walking around, supposedly intellectually observing a lifestyle which I have lived.

Because of their awareness of existing problems, the future teachers felt that they also had an idea of what *should* be happening. Stu, Ben, and Clive saw the situation this way:

The primary crisis in black education is one of quality. The inferior quality of education in black schools has had a drastic effect on the IQ score of young Afro-Americans. . . . It is safe to say that many black school children are unable to learn because they are not taught.

Cal's reaction, however, was much more emotional:

We reside in a nation of satiated citizens. People are surfeited with displeasure at the system which allows them to be socially, or economically ravished. Although the rape is committed against all of the racial and ethnic segments of this society, its historical atrocities against the black man demonstrate the savageness and contradiction—the double standard—by which man can coexist and by which societies can advance and grow to grandure while preying on members who are made the victims of that growth. When the predator has become comfortable, relaxed, and benevolent to its victim, it is then time for the victim to begin his quest for recognition.

Freddi believed that the fault lay with the way black children felt about themselves. The way they had been treated by others, mostly whites, had made them feel worthless:

Some evidence suggests that many black children have a very low self-concept. In a study . . . black children were given the opportunity to choose between a black doll and a white doll to play with. The majority of the black children chose a white doll. Why? I say it is because the schools have not provided an adequate curriculum that reflects the truth about black people.

The Chicanos in the group attributed the injustices to Chicanitos to the schools' disregard of Mexican-American language and culture:

For the most part, schools are detrimental to Chicano children because they so often ignore and reject the cultural heritage and language of the Chicano. It is our feeling that prior to the school experience, most Chicanitos are psychologically healthy, intact, and stable. Once in school, cultural conflicts gradually develop causing the children to begin to question their homes, their families, their values and ultimately themselves. In essence, the children begin to doubt all that is meaningful to them.

Through the program, the participants sought answers to the third question, "How can we make it happen?" As a group of individual persons committed to action, they were eager to find solutions. For this reason they saw as most meaningful the curriculum projects they developed and the teaching strategies with which they struggled to become proficient. Because they were seekers themselves, they could understand the necessity of learning to ask questions of children that required thoughtful answers. They saw the significance of helping children to ask questions too, as well as to give answers. They knew that children should be able to cope with strange and new situations. They saw role playing as a way that children could know and understand their own feelings; simulation was a tool that would bring the real world into the classroom. By freeing the children's drive for creativity, the new teachers could help them to develop alternative modes for expressing themselves. By learning the steps of operant conditioning and programmed learning as well, the prospective teachers were increasing the number of tools available for helping children learn and develop. In all, the curriculum seminar gave them a variety of ways to design their minischools during the summer. This challenge was always foremost in their minds.

Because, as the spring wore on, participants increasingly felt the urgency of this challenge, they became impatient with generalized solutions. Additionally, they were looking for immediate answers to the in-school instructional problems they were encountering during a variety of field experiences. Therefore, the seminar format was abandoned in response to a need for consultation and planning time with black and Chicano advisors. These advisors helped with minischool planning, and they later served as operational consultants to the minischool groups.

The groups, which spontaneously rallied around issues of common concern, not only planned and established the six minischools, they also emerged as little "learning communities" in which problems associated with the issues could be attacked. In these small interest-based groups, the graduate students created mechanisms for integrating their past and present experiences with plans for the months ahead. "Present experiences" included both course work and field activities. As they mobilized and reinforced their biases in cliques of mutual concern, the participants had a sense that they were "getting it together" for the major task confronting them: implementing minischool programs during the summer.

The preplanned program had been structured on the assumption that by sharing experiences and perceptions with each other, the participants would discover areas that would command the attention of the entire group. The concept of a "Learning Community" was employed to suggest the appropriateness of the group's developing its own resources in addressing matters of general interest and in seeking solutions to shared problems. The basic program plan included this concept in order to provide an arena in which the peer group might further define the program and shape it to meet challenges identified by the participants themselves. Both their course work and their field experiences were expected to contribute to this process of identification.

Problems arising in the course of the program—especially those emerging from field experiences—were expected to have commonalities. The program planners anticipated that, when together, participants would share experiences and perceptions through which a bond would develop among them. Through a communal effort, the participants were expected to experience the value of a collegial approach to problem solving that would motivate them to draw upon institutional resources. The very name "Learning Community" suggested the following ideas: that a wide variety of learning opportunities were available; that the group enjoyed a measure of autonomy; and that initiative for independent action lay with the group.

The learning community was expected to serve not only as a forum, but also as an instrument through which the participants might integrate all parts of the program during both semesters of the academic year. The learning community was to be student directed and its thrust was to be determined by their needs that were not being met in other learning situations. Given the responsibility and the resources for assessing, shaping, and refining their own program, the future teachers were expected to be actively involved in the process of planning for their professional growth. The program staff was available to facilitate this planning.

The participants, however, were not easily manipulated into conformity to a prestructured program concept. They moved in sometimes predictable and sometimes erratic relationships to each other and to the principal thrust of the program. The result was a fluid learning community rather than one frozen into a solid state.

Among the preterns there was general apathy toward consolidating interests and expending energy to make "a group." Instead, each participant drew upon very personal experiences for motivation toward "worthy" goals. Worth was defined by using very personal criteria. When paths crossed, the participants offered no objection. When they diverged, that was acceptable too. However, the students felt strongly that time spent on an analysis of these trends was time wasted, and they did not want to devote themselves to planning for common interests. They regarded such engagements as entanglements that would frustrate direct attack upon critical problems. These problems were enmeshed in a web of social and psychological complexities already. Intensive involvement with the group could only complicate matters and create diversions. When purposes were held in common, it was fortuitous. Chance occurrences revealed shared concerns; then subgroups formed. Many of the initial field experiences that were planned for the group resulted in alliances. Ultimately, these became learning communities and the planning groups for individual minischools.

In preparation for the minischools, the year's activities were geared to move gradually from broad, extensive experiences, toward focused, concentrated involvements. These culminated in a four- to six-week spring practicum period when the preterns taught full time *in classrooms of their own selection.* During the prepracticum experience, members of the group were expected to spend an average of fifteen to twenty hours a week in communities served by an identified school. Participants were encouraged to alternate school-based activities emphasizing focused involvement with those that provided more wide-ranging exploration. The suggested shifts of pace and focus were intended to offer choice-points for further activity and involvement, along with opportunity for reflection and evaluation.

Introductory experiences were planned to coordinate the curriculum studies seminar and the field activities. Program participants needed to gain a broad view if they were to answer the question of "What's happening?" and were to discover some tentative answers to the questions of "What should be happening?" and "How do we make it happen?" The first activity was a quick and wide-ranging tour of the Los Angeles area in order to get an overview of a mega-lopolis. A three-week program of study trips into different urban areas then offered a broad assortment of experiences as well as models for later field exploration in communities close at hand. During their visits to the city, the participants looked at grassroots organizations, they spoke with representatives within a predominant-ly Mexican-American community, a black community, and one with a "mixed" ethnic and racial population that was undergoing the adjustments required by re-cent integration. Attempts to assess the tenor of "the people" were followed by observation of the established society's institutions and by an accompanying dia-logue with its officialdom. Time was divided about equally between "the com-munity" and "the schools," with school visitations in each area extending from nursery to continuation schools. Organizations, representing interests and politi-cal processes ranging beyond the community in which they were located, were included in the itinerary; among these were public health agencies, police sta-tions, teachers' unions, Head Starts, and juvenile and housing authorities.

The participants' responses to these introductory experiences were as dif-ferent as their own backgrounds and depended to a large extent upon them. Some of the participants, whose life experiences had brought them into inti-mate contact with the realities under investigation, regarded the planned pro-gram as superficial and superfluous, and they caused some of their fellows to view scheduled activities with a skeptical eye. Most of the group withheld judgment, however, and participated in the inner-city visits with varied and fluctuating amounts of enthusiasm, depending upon how closely a particular activity touched a specialized interest or concern.

The faculty had requested that the students try to refrain from identifying with young people in particular categories—especially categories associated with age. Experiences were planned so that the future teachers would see educational influences as a continuum in the dynamic process of individual human growth. They were encouraged to "hang loose" and explore widely before narrowing the area and the range of their involvement. The unique advantage offered by a program designed to extend to participants the opportunity to earn credentials for either elementary or secondary teaching was primarily an advantage of per-spective. A program for developing teacher leaders at any level of public school-ing from kindergarten through secondary was posited on the assumption that teachers of children or youth at any particular grade or level would be better teachers of the young if they did not see that grade or level as disjunctive. It was also assumed that teachers of children at any grade or level would be better teachers of those children if their own experience with children were not isolated between two neighboring points on the educational continuum. Also, every effort was made to provide the participants with experiences that would cast light on the importance of continuity between home and school experi-ences.

Following the excursions that were arranged to highlight home, school, and community relationships in a metropolitan region some forty' or fifty miles from the campus, independent field exploration in nearby areas was encouraged. The guidelines for field exploration emphasized that this period was to be a time of fluidity between in-school and out-of-school community involvement. A memorandum addressed to the students after the conclusion of the Los Angeles visits advised them as follows with regard to their locally based activities:

> *Try to see lots of things, talk to lots of people, and to get the big picture with regard to the community. You should strive for an idea of the process of schooling which children in the community experience across a span of twelve to fourteen years, and how that process relates to the reality of life in that community.*

The participants were urged to involve themselves in the functions of community-based organizations and in the process to develop a relationship with a child that would help them to see the community and the schools from a personal and family perspective.

The participants had come to the program, however, because they perceived the role of the teacher as central to social change. They chose, therefore, to work primarily in classrooms and not in "communities" as such. They were intense about their work with children and tended to get deeply involved with them before gaining the recommended broad view through an extensive experience in school communities. Commitment to a particular ethnic or age group that had grown out of prior experiences caused participants to target their activities almost from the outset. Few were interested in the blurred complexities of the big picture. It was unmanageable. Most sought to fulfill the demands of a predetermined and well-defined charge to themselves; they wanted to learn how to manage things within a circumscribed arena.

When they arrived in September many participants had already established the target groups for their involvement: kindergarteners, adolescents, black, brown, or troubled youngsters. These participants were impatient to acquire the management and teaching skills they needed in order to do important things with the young people they were most concerned about. They wanted to do it all "Now!" Some attempted just that. Two participants, Mia and the woman who later left the program, persuasively sought approval to teach together in a Follow Through kindergarten where a bicultural-bilingual model was being developed. Their experiences, like those of others among their peers, became more intensive, rather than more varied. Many participants chose to work in a particular public school situation because the children needed help, rather than because the situation was instructive to themselves or because a particular teacher could suggest useful ways of helping children to learn. The prospective teachers did not always wait for official approval before increasing classroom involvement to full time "teaching." They were eager to teach children and youth, and many used the entire year of preparation to do just that. However, the participants learned something about themselves in the process, and all of them regarded the practicum experience as the most useful in preparation for minischool operation and for program implementation. With regard to their preparation for full-time classroom teaching, they viewed the practicum as second in importance only to minischool experiences.

The importance of mutual confidence between preservice and inservice teachers to a fully satisfactory experimental teaching experience was a matter upon which participants and program personnel agreed fully. The expectation that this goal was possible through an exploratory approach to placement in classrooms became an issue only when a different view was held by school district personnel. Some district representatives regarded "practice teaching" as an orientation period for a particular job in a particular circumstance. While a buyers' job market would have made a decision to comply with school district placement understandable, and perhaps justifiable, the students were generally unwilling to "sell out" to security, however. Asked if they would rather "play it safe" or take their chances with a situation that seemed desirable but not so likely to provide a job the following year, the preterns expressed a profound preference for working in situations of their own choosing.

While some of the participants sustained a year-long commitment to a particular school or classroom that for them was, or developed into, a practicum experience, more than half of the group conducted an actual search directed toward ultimately finding "the right situation." Generally there was elation expressed after its discovery. Not infrequently disenchantment and even depression followed, as the subtleties of in-school relationships became apparent and the reality of an involvement was seen as other than that to which they aspired. Since *they* had chosen the situation, however, the discrepancy between the ideal and the real was particularly meaningful to the aspiring teachers, and the opportunity for significant learning was great, albeit painful.

Only two students—Freddi and Cal—enjoyed an intensive involvement apparently free from anxiety. Freddi experienced almost no tensions between her felt needs and programmatic expectations; Cal found that there were many points of conflict and resolved the problem by virtually ignoring programmatic aspects unless doing otherwise suited his purposes. Idealistic regarding what *should* be, uncertain of their own competence to effect it, and impatient to acquire the competencies they sought, many others were often anxious and sometimes deeply discouraged about the practicum experience. Group "control" and classroom management were of central concern to many.

Observation of participants in the field indicated many commonalities in their perceptions and pointed to the myriad issues associated with locating a "good" practicum situation. Not uncommonly the very characteristics upon which a choice was based were later perceived to be functional constraints upon the participants' options. The importance to them of locating and working in classrooms of their choice, and the fact that their period of intensive participation was of critical significance during the year's activities, is documented in detail elsewhere.[1]

Subsequent to the practicum period, eleven of the fifteen summarized the experience in writing as they were requested to do. They indicated the meaning that this period of intensive involvement held for them. Three of those who had shown considerable anxiety during the practicum stated that it had been *the most useful* program experience to date:

. . . It was the most significant experience of the program in terms of what I take my needs to be. Ms. _____ and I spent much time talking together, spinning theories, watching kids, trying out things. In terms of seeing someone consistently deal with kids such that they were forced to look at what they were doing, I found Ms. _____ to be remarkable. I feel I began to gain some competence with the kids in this regard.

. . . I think that this practicum was the most important experience of my first year. I respected my master teacher both as a sympathetic friend and highly competent professional. She spoke openly to me about black problems, aspirations, and thereby helped me gain greater security as far as my understanding of black people. . . . She is at the same time a highly structured teacher. Although I sometimes felt restricted by this, I also learned a great deal about children's needs for security, for an environment in which they feel important and able to work.

. . . I feel that my practicum has been the most meaningful and worthwhile educational experience I've had in the program this far. It has proven to me that the most effective teacher training method is on-the-job experience. . . . It gave me the opportunity to find out what I was like in the classroom, what I needed to know and improve on, the potential I had. It put me in a situation where I had to wrestle with the problems of my students, the problems created by some of the faculty I was working with, and those conjured up by myself.

Only one of the responding participants did not find the practicum experience a worthwhile one:

It is hard for me to work in a simulated situation. Basically, I felt as though my role in the classroom was hampered, not because of any restrictions that Ms. _____ put on me, but because I respected her position and tried not to interfere with her. I had a lot of ideas that I suppressed because I put myself in her place. It would have been like this in any classroom where I would be subject to a master teacher. . . . I truly believe that for me, a master teacher is practically useless.

This student went on the say that the experience of substitute teaching provided the challenge of "a real situation with no attempt to spare the hell that a teacher goes through . . . no attempt to glamorize a truly deplorable profession."

Other participants reported that their practicum involvement contributed to confidence that they would survive as teachers. Most mentioned the things they had learned about children (". . . all are individuals and must be approached as individuals . . .") and about themselves (". . . highlighted my weaknesses—art, drama, and dance"; "I learned to be more patient"). The participants described how the experience had made them aware of the necessity for planning and for flexibility. It also provided opportunity to "get the feel" of a particular learning environment well enough to evaluate it in terms of their own experience and that of children:

. . . I saw clearly how difficult it would be to institute an open and self-directed classroom with a group of kids who are used to a very traditional and teacher-oriented classroom.

. . . I was able to grasp a broad understanding of an Open Classroom. . . . I could see how the children in this class responded to an open environment created by them and their teacher.

. . . Having to adjust to Mr. ____'s class structure and his very strict utilization of time segments, I almost viscerally reacted negatively. All of my own school years with all of the impatience I had felt came back to me. It convinced me that I didn't want such a structured environment.

One participant concluded her report with the statement, "In summary, I now have a frame of reference from which to work in strengthening my competence as a teacher." These words seemed to summarize, also, the general group feeling with regard to the usefulness of the practicum experience.

This period of intensive work in public school classrooms stood in intimate relationship to later interim involvements that some participants courted and developed in the period between the practicum and the beginning of the summer program. Cal and Maxine were given permission to engage in substitute teaching on a limited basis. Sylvia sought increased insight into educationally related problems of which classroom teachers are often unaware, and she became engaged in volunteer counseling at a free clinic in a nearby community. A school district's offer to Ben of a part-time position teaching adolescent patients at a psychiatric hospital was sanctioned because it promised to provide him an experience that would bring his previous involvements into more objective perspective. Several students sustained involvement at their practicum sites while getting different views of it through participation in special programs, such as cross-age teaching.

A variety of additional activities during the spring seemed to cast the intensive practicum period into larger perspective. The participants attended conferences and workshops, visited schools and centers of educational activity based on widely different philosophical orientations; they examined "programs" instituted for various purposes; they talked to administrators, curriculum consultants, teachers, parents, and children. Wide-ranging scouting expeditions took some of them into Nevada, and over half the group spent a week in the San Francisco bay region looking into innovative programs in that area. With elapsed time and intervening experience, the participants were increasingly able to evaluate those situations in which they had been involved earlier. As Helga said after extensive observation during the late spring, "Now I realize how really bad (i.e., rigid) my practicum classroom really was."

In choosing their own situations for intensive in-school experiences, all but Boyd selected classrooms with a large number of minority children and except for his, cooperating teachers were black or Chicano. However, just as choices of situations for practicum involvement were consonant with individual interests, concerns, and priorities, the fact was also apparent that specific outcomes varied. Clearly though, most of the participants grew and developed during the course of their field experiences. They came to look at themselves and at learning environments with different lenses than the ones used when they entered the program. For most, their perceptions of chosen situations shifted considerably during the course of the practicum, and the future teachers were increasingly sensitive to the complexity of school-staff-community relationships. Some saw a need for further observation in schools; others felt that they had served their apprenticeship and resisted further participatory activity in public school classrooms.

While the practicum period was one of stimulation and excitement in teaching, it was also one of tension and frustration. Limited authority meant limited opportunity for influence. As Sylvia stated when discussing possibilities for home visitation in relation to a child's difficulties: "It would be presumptuous. I'm not his teacher."

Most of the aspiring teachers experienced considerable difficulty working in classrooms controlled by others, while trying to adapt their ideas to the expectations of both teachers and children. Still, many persisted in the effort, for in these classrooms they could be in meaningful contact with significant numbers of children from the particular groups or with the particular problems that had captured their interests. Ultimately, these interests were what separated the participants into the subgroups that established minischools along such widely differing lines.

With the approach of summer, diffuse minischool plans required definition in the form of proposals. These outlined specific objectives and the activities planned to meet them. There was a frantic, almost panicky, flurry of activity as all-out effort was made to "get things shaped up." On their arrival in September, the future teachers felt aggrieved that they were not to start their little schools immediately and run them all year. In May, many wondered how they could be ready and have them operating by June!

5 Large Tasks for Little Schools

The proposed minischools had one purpose as far as the participants in the Teacher Leader Program were concerned: to provide children and young people with effective, appropriate learning experiences. The program planners saw the minischool's function differently: to provide embryonic teachers with a medium for their own professional development as decisionmakers. Either way, the minischool concept exemplified the program's problem-solving approach to rectifying inequities. It assumed a degree of social awareness and competence in teaching that the academic year's program had been designed to develop. The minischool programs would not only test the participants and their ideas, but the very experience itself would be part of the process of preparation for full-time teaching. The ultimate objective was development of the participants' ability to identify and analyze a problem, to hypothesize about solutions, and to test alternatives. The minischools required the preterns to establish defensible goals, to operationalize them, and to evaluate their programs and themselves in the light of feedback and outcomes.

If the practicum experience was anxiety producing because of situational constraints, the minischool experience was threatening because the possibilities for achievement were open ended. The participants' freedom to shape a relevant and viable program was limited only by the money they were each allotted ($346.00), temporal factors (mornings for six weeks), and, most threatening of all, their own perceptions, judgments, and creativity. Although they acknowledged their responsibility toward expenditure of funds and for justifying and meeting their program goals, emotionally the participants held themselves accountable for the lives of children—for making a difference in those lives. This commitment was a large one, even without full responsibility in decision making; *with* complete autonomy, it was "heavy," heady, and exciting. There could be no scapegoating: There were no principals, no curriculum requirements, no code books on which to blame program shortcomings. The participants could select their schools' populations, their staffs, their housing, their programs, their activities, and their materials. The line between "challenge" and "threat" was a slender one and not entirely stable.

In each school was compounded a mixture of enthusiasm, hope, and apprehension. However, the minischools were as different as those who established them. Each school was a reflection of the philosophies and styles of those involved. In the case of group projects, they also reflected the dynamics manifested within particular groups.

51

Each of the groups was self-selected on the basis of shared social and ideological commitments. The process of role separation within groups varied. In some cases it was based on competencies and interests. In others, agreement seemed to rest upon unarticulated notions regarding appropriate power relations. Whether they were achieved through conscious or unconscious processes, these understandings appeared to be functional. They might have been attributed to the fact that each minischool staff was engaged in a common task and that each person had an equal investment in its outcome.

Despite this generally harmonious climate, there were some differences among team members that generated enough interpersonal tension to produce anxiety. These differences, which might be identified as incongruity of styles and approaches, seemed to strengthen their minischools, however. Their individual abilities, skills, and perspectives appeared to complement each other, to increase options, and to promote general flexibility.

The record of minischool development reveals both the ambitiousness of the participants and the scope of the concept. The participants confronted an array of problems: complex community social relationships, including factions competing for power and recognition; criteria for admission of students, with concomitant problems related to exclusion; arrangements for a supporting staff; transportation and logistics; working out arrangements for reciprocity with cooperating agencies; communication with and involvement of parents and the immediate community; public relations with the wider community; and environmental problems associated with situational constraints. In the six minischools, varied solution to these and other problems were found.

The little schools directly served some one hundred and fifty students; about sixty more benefitted indirectly through tutoring activities that engaged the students of one minischool. There were between fifteen and thirty students in each minischool, and the six minischools spanned an age range of about fourteen years. There was one preschool group, and two groups were drawn from high school populations. The other three minischools served children of elementary school age. All student groups were multi-aged within these broad categories.

There were two programs for black students and one for Mexican-American children. The other three projects were not so homogeneously grouped, and of these one student group was specifically selected for a racial mix.

Three projects made use of their Mexican-American children's home language and culture. Two of these had at least one bilingual teacher. The little school serving Mexican-American children exclusively, had three bilinguals on its four-teacher team.

Although one of the six projects was a forty-five minute drive from the Claremont campus, the others were ten to twenty minutes away, within neighboring communities. All little schools were housed in the facilities of established organizations: Two were located in churches, two in the community rooms of public housing projects for low-income families; and two in public school buildings. Three of the minischool groups obtained state attendance money for local school districts. Through such political strategies, the participants gained support from "the establishment," which legitimized each project to the prospective clientele and enabled the staff to obtain needed facilities, materials, and, in one case, high school credit for the young people involved.

All minischool programs were intended to improve their students' academic performance and all included better self-concepts among their goals. Curricular emphases varied greatly, however, as did the means selected for the accomplishment of major objectives. Targeted were understandings related to the following: social interrelationships in urban and community settings; concepts of time and space; cultural identity; and intergroup power relationships. The hopes and expectations that in six short weeks changes might be effected with regard to such broad and important categories meant that the little schools were charged with performing very large tasks, indeed. The means employed in them focused upon: inquiry processes in the natural and social sciences; traditional didactic instruction; activities in the dramatic and expressive arts (with emphasis upon language skills); and primary experiences that capitalized upon local community resources as well as field excursions into the wider world.

The preterns regarded parent and other adult participation as especially important. Their approaches to fostering parent involvement ranged from requiring a commitment of parents enrolling their children to simply inviting participation because of attractive programs. And the participation ranged from minimal and perfunctory to extensive and spontaneous. Additionally, many minischools were helped by such volunteers as high school students, professionals, and civic leaders from the schools' communities. More than half were older youngsters for whom participation may also be regarded as a learning experience. One minischool had a "student teacher"—a participant from a more traditional teacher preparation program—on its staff. The students of another were afternoon "teachers" of over sixty children living in the area surrounding the minischool. Four minischools had the services of paid aides.

While the matters requiring consideration were many, as long as the participants were simply preparing for their little schools, they could deal with issues in a relatively systematic and objective manner, as they arose. Once their schools were operational, all that changed, however. Mornings were filled with action, with confrontations, with myriad complex problems. Each crisis seemed to require immediate action without the time needed to think about the conceptual schemes that they had identified as guidelines for making decisions. In anticipation of this, afternoons had been designed to include moments of relaxation along with opportunities to examine and to reflect upon the morning events. Time in which to reevaluate priorities and to alter directions was recognized as critically important. But, so also was time for the re-creation of perspectives. This was necessary to reducing anxiety and to effective functioning under stress.

Resources of the graduate school were available to aid in the ongoing process of redirecting, planning, and preparation. Consultants were "on call" to work with participants, on curriculum, and other concerns. The faculty and staff, who were also involved in the regular teacher preparation programs, were on campus most of the time. As part of their program the group participated in many of the twenty-plus summer offerings of teacher education's basic sequence.

In traditional programs a fixed curriculum schedule is prescribed for prospective teachers. With some latitude, students take courses and work in them for a given amount of time, such as a quarter, a semester, or another time module. The program participants' studies were not so rigidly organized. Instead, as a question arose in a minischool, the "teachers" were free to seek answers to it: "How do you use experience stories to teach reading?" "What sources are there for high interest–low difficulty books about the city?" "Where can free scrap materials be obtained that the children can use for collages?"

Through a personalized contracting process, these summer studies were given a minimal structure. Early in June, with minischool operation uppermost in their minds, the participants established goals to which they committed themselves. They also identified resources that might be used to achieve their objectives. The parties to these contracts agreed upon evidence that would be presented to show objectives had been accomplished.

Since the coordinator had worked closely with the participants the previous year, she knew both their strengths and weaknesses and was able to give counsel as the needs of each were assessed. Contracting was a process of negotiation between the coordinator, the participants, and the instructors. In many ways it was fluid and ongoing, since there was opportunity at any time during the summer to renegotiate. About half took advantage of this arrangement and revised their original plans. When a change occurred, it was usually because participants had overestimated what they could accomplish in such a short time.

The aspirations of individual participants were generally high. With the exception of a few who seemed to have given only perfunctory attention to specific ways by which they might achieve their purposes, most participants came to the conference table having thoughtfully considered not only their interests, but also their areas of weakness and strength. Objectives ranged from the broad and general to the focused and specific:

To explore art and media as the needs arise in the minischool;

To acquire social studies concepts applicable at any grade level;

To help children develop an awareness of the forces that shape the lives of people;

To find easy-reading books for children that will help them appreciate differences among individual people and groups.

In the contracting situation most participants demonstrated a clear awareness of their needs in relation to both their minischool undertakings and their
future teaching responsibilities. The gamut and number of their objectives
revealed, along with their overall ambition, the hopes they brought with them
to their summer studies.

Most of the participants felt positive about the concept of contracting. They
saw it as supportive of their morning work in the minischools. It enabled them
to obtain information and services that were needed and immediately applicable.
Their studies in areas of the curriculum took on a relevancy that made it easier
to perform the tasks they had set for themselves:

*The idea of negotiating contracts allowed for us to get into things that we
thought interesting and valuable. No matter how important or relevant a course
is, if a person is not ready for the material or not interested in it then it's sense-
less to be required to take it. Providing a curriculum which offered true freedom
of choice was a positive step away from the hyprocrisy that too often exists. . . .*

As usual, however, no consensus could be obtained within the group. Some
participants did not like the contracting process because they were not used to
it, because they felt it was unnecessarily coercive, or because they saw it as a
device by which a white Anglo institution could manipulate the powerless. The
issue of power relationships between participants and the graduate institution
was an ever-present one for some preterns.

However, tensions associated with power relationships were not limited to
those between individual participants and the institution of higher education
with which they were associated. Because of the maneuvering for power that
characterized the era, the participants constantly experienced personal anxiety
along with tensions among themselves. They were especially sensitive to emerging racial and ethnic identities, which created not only outcroppings of dogma,
but also undercurrents of uncertainty. The interpersonal dynamics affected
were unpredictable. They influenced most choices and moved as a constant
threat to rapport among those who sought a smooth passage in their work
together.

Additionally, all the participants seemed to experience a conflict with
regard to the open-closed, freedom-control continuum when they were considering alternatives for structuring teaching-learning environments. Even when
the preterns had decided on a course of action, they continued to scrutinize
their commitment to it by checking decisions against the ideas of other persons.
The tensions caused by this uncertainty only added to the anxiety produced
by the risk taking inherent in the minischool ventures. A major problem central
to each of the minischool projects was that of discovering, maintaining, and
stretching the limits of that optimum balance between risk and security, anxiety
and comfort, mobility and stability. The participants sought solutions to this

problem in different ways, depending upon individual and group points of departure.

High program priority was given to processes of problem solving. Participants were encouraged to maintain daily logs for this purpose, to sit with their staffs in regular feedback and planning sessions, and to otherwise engage in formative assessment. Beyond these suggestions, they were required to evaluate their projects in summative reports, and the minischools figure prominently in critiques that participants wrote relative to their studies in the program.

While most of the participants stated that as a consequence of the summer program they would be more effective teachers, limited time and energy also resulted in frustrations. What many participants were capable of achieving in six weeks did not measure up to their own aspirations. Although many problems with which they grappled were rooted in the lives of the young people with whom they chose to work, the preterns' choices were guided by their concerns with particular issues. The programs they created were shaped by very personal perceptions of these issues.[1]

Each minischool endeavor was an attempt to answer questions and to solve problems that threatened the core of participants' identities, as well as their concepts of themselves in the teacher's role. Some of the issues were clearly identified by the participants. Others were less apparent, were unarticulated, and perhaps were even below the participants' level of awareness. These can only be inferred through observations of the process of schoolmaking. An examination of the hidden curriculum that energized each participant reveals that the minischools were loaded with personal significance.

Commitment to the minischools drained the participants, and they found attending to matters that were not immediately useful was difficult. Their morning responsibilities weighed heavily upon them, and the potential teacher leaders found themselves almost totally preoccupied with meeting the day-to-day needs associated with programs at the little schools. There, educational processes went on, simultaneously, on two levels. As children learned, the schoolmakers were becoming prepared for classroom teaching. For them, their teacher education took place, primarily, on the site of the six minischools: Live Oak, the Black School, La Escuelita, Las Palmas, Ramona, and the Urban Studies Workshop.

Part III
The Minischools

6

Live Oak

Freddi's prior experience as director of the Teen-Post had given her a clear indication of children's psychological and academic needs that no agency was successfully serving. While working with the teenagers, she observed that their lively young brothers and sisters spent lack-luster summer days without constructive activities or guidance. There was so much they might be doing and learning, if only the opportunity could be provided. Freddi saw the Teacher Leader Program as a source of that opportunity. However, because this community that was familiar to her was some distance from the Claremont campus, she knew she would be unable to enlist the support of her fellows in initiating a project there, and she made no attempt to do so.

From the first time the participants met in the fall, Freddi's intuition appeared sound. Throughout the year, her judgments struck a responsive chord within her peer group and among her instructors. When it was necessary for her to conceptualize her ideas, however, she lacked the facility to elaborate the unarticulated notions that she had about teaching and learning. Anxious about projects that involved systematic planning, Freddi neeeded personal encouragement, the pressure of time constraints, and insistent demands to complete assigned tasks. Her tentativeness was especially apparent when she was required to submit the written minischool proposal, a prerequisite to approval and funding of each project.

The proposal that Freddi initially submitted was not impressive, but it did reflect her sensitivity about what would be "right for kids." Hers was a guarded enthusiasm that needed both emotional and rational support in order to flower. Her approach was: "I have this idea, but dare I follow it through?"

She wanted to help preschool children in the low-income black neighborhood. She wanted them to discover that they were capable of taking charge of their own lives. She believed that this could be done if they were given responsibility for ordering their own learning environment. However, she wondered whether she should trust her intuition enough to base an entire project upon it. Even in the moments when she was certain that she was right, Freddi questioned that, alone, she could "carry it off" and bring about the program and the outcomes she hoped for.

She knew her ideas were well founded because they arose from her observations of the children with whom she wanted to work. However, she admitted to needing help organizing her thoughts. Given that help, Freddi was able to elaborate the rationale for her minischool program. She planned activities based

59

on defensible social and psychological principles. Then, with a conceptual framework in mind, she was able to relate her own afternoon summer studies to the goals of her morning project.

The church that housed the Teen-Post was chosen as the site for Freddi's minischool since it had many advantages. It stood adjacent to the area where the children lived. Transportation to and from school would be no problem for parents since many of the children could walk to the minischool with older siblings. Also, in a sprawling city of over 100,000 inhabitants, the Live Oak section where the church was located included shops and other businesses that were accessible for little excursions into the community. Short walking trips could provide an experiential base for other curricular activities. Additionally, there was a museum within strolling distance.

The facility that was available to the pretern was a large, sunny classroom equipped with child-size tables and chairs, shelves, materials for play and construction, room dividers, and a piano. Freddi could also make use of a spacious social hall for music, dance, and other activities that required free movement or the use of special facilities; besides a stage for dramatic play, it contained equipment for cooking and sewing. Freddi detailed all these advantages in her minischool proposal and then added a pragmatic note: "Another is that the facility was offered rent free."

Familiar with the Teen-Post participants, Freddi knew she could count on them to help, and the proposal she drew up in the spring reflected her intention to promote the teenagers' involvement in cross-age teaching. This would be to their benefit, as well as to that of the younger children, she noted. The pretern requested and received five Neighborhood Youth Corps workers to serve as paraprofessionals in her minischool. Since they were paid from another source, she did not have to allocate funds for staff from her small budget.

The inclusion of another adult in her minischool proved to be a fortuitous decision when a subsequent family emergency temporarily drew Freddi away from the project. The woman, who was active in the NAACP, volunteered to serve as Freddi's assistant because she was also interested in trying "new" ways of teaching. She was chairman of the Teen-Post board of directors and a teacher in a metropolitan school district. Freddi regarded this teacher's experience as an asset to the program.

In her minischool proposal, Freddi established the roles that the teenagers were to fill. They were to help assess, plan, guide, and stimulate their charges. The primary minischool goal was to develop the children's perception of themselves as competent learners who could ask relevant questions and speculate about their answers. In her objectives for the children, Freddi revealed her desire that they be able to express their ideas well. In the initial planning, her minischool curriculum was heavily weighted toward the language and graphic arts and toward activities involving music. As she reflected upon and elaborated activities she recognized the necessity for firsthand experience as the raw material basic to self-expression and productivity.

Freddi viewed her proposed field trips and science experiences as necessary to priming a flow of creativity on the part of the children. However, she did not regard creativity as an end in itself. Her goals clearly showed her concern that the children find in the minischool program a route to self-mastery and self-esteem. By equipping young black children with the basic skills for social escalation in contemporary life, Freddi sought to improve substantially their self-concepts. While she held high hopes for the outcomes of a six-week program, she also was aware that her aspiration level might be unrealistic. At times she was plunged into despair by the contrast between practical constraints and the range of her own vision. The scope of that vision is documented in one of the objectives Freddi established for herself during the summer contracting process: ". . . to provide opportunities for children to discover causal relationships and to experience themselves as competent manipulators of their environment, able to predict and control outcomes."

Freddi became convinced that exploration into natural phenomena would provide the best opportunity for the children to develop their cognitive powers. Through involvement in a series of scientific experiments, they would be able "to formulate verbally ideas, assumptions, and theories about their experiences." She arrived at this conclusion despite limited personal knowledge about the field of science or of how to teach it. But, being both practical and without pretense—without either false modesty or false pride—Freddi acknowledged her shortcomings and asked for help in this area. Since "science" and the strategies for teaching it were not to be part of the program of curriculum studies until the following academic year when the participants would be teaching interns in public schools, Claremont's resources—both material and human—were made available to Freddi, and she enthusiastically utilized them as time would permit.

To facilitate her recruitment of children, Freddi talked to some of the parents living in a low-income housing project near Live Oak. The project housed some one hundred and fifty families, about half of which were on welfare. She enlisted their help:

I told them I wanted to experiment with some teaching ideas which may be helpful to me when I started teaching in a regular public school. I told them some of my ideas for teaching reading, math, and science. I also told them that my program would include field trips to the zoo, park, library, and beach. I explained that although this would be a new experience for me, I believed my program would help increase the children's skills in reading, writing, math, and science. I also stated the children would have fun.

The resultant group of potential participants was reduced to manageable proportions by two requirements that Freddi established for enrollment. One was the requirement of parental involvement for one hour a week. With this expectation, the pretern hoped to develop a closer alliance between home activities and those in the minischool as well as to increase parents' investment in educational outcomes. The second requirement was an even more arbitrary limitation. She decreed that no more than two children per family would be eligible for participation. From a large family herself, Freddi was well aware that sibling competition might pose problems that could interfere with progress toward established goals.

The appropriateness of her program's mission was confirmed for Freddi when she paid home visits to the eighteen youngsters she recruited for her minischool. She found herself asking how people with little understanding of temporal relationships could plan adequately for the future. Many specific objectives for the minischool curriculum emerged in response to questions posed by the children: "When will our school start?" "How long is three days?" "When will tomorrow come?" These questions heightened Freddi's awareness of the importance of helping the children develop a time perspective. She hoped to help them see themselves as capable of making things happen. As a prerequisite she felt that it was necessary for them "to understand *when* things happen."

A partial solution to this problem was to develop a daily program. Again Freddi took her cues from the children instead of imposing adult standards upon them. She watched the youngsters in order to learn about their natural patterns of activity and to match the rhythms of the morning program to the dispositions of the children:

After two days of observing the children, I planned a schedule that would be helpful to me in teaching them time relationship. I wanted the children to become familiar with time in relation to their classroom activities. . . . I wanted to provide a program whereby each child could learn at his own pace and feel good about his learning and himself as a person.

Freddi also sought to help children bring the physical environment under their control:

I wanted to instill in each child a sense that the entire classroom belonged to him, his peers, and the teachers. He, therefore, had to take some responsibility for initiating and carrying out activities that interested him. I wanted each child to know that the teachers would help him in his endeavor to acquire the skills of his interest.

In my minischool, emphasis was placed on the scientific method or process—the scientist's way of thinking about problems and solving them, rather than on the acquisition of facts for their own sake. Experience through observation and manipulation enabled the children to gain a better insight of what is actually taking place in their environment. My goal was to facilitate active self-directed learners. Participation, I believe, helped them develop competent modes of inquiry and become involved with science as a process. More important, it helped them develop an awareness of their powers to be masters over their environment.

Freddi extended this orientation to the organization of the classroom and the materials that contributed to the program's implementation. The children became active participants in the process of ordering their objective world. While examining available data, they were able to "see, hear, feel, and otherwise experience in a direct way," at the same time as they categorized things and reflected upon relationships within their immediate environment. Freddi helped the children organize equipment and space according to functional criteria. In recounting the events that launched her minischool program, Freddi explained that she put into boxes all the materials she planned to use; she took these boxes into the classroom and placed them in the middle of the floor:

When the children arrived the first day there were no preplanned activities waiting for them to carry out. I explained to the children that all of the school supplies were in the boxes and I wanted each of them to plan and place things where they wanted them. I told them to work for fifteen minutes taking the things out of the boxes, looking at them and discussing them with one another. I explained that at the end of the fifteen minutes a timer would ring. They were to come and sit on the rug when they heard the timer.

At the end of the fifteen minutes, the children returned to the rug. I told them that I wanted them to talk for fifteen minutes about the kinds of materials they found in the boxes. Richie immediately stated, "You didn't give us time enough to finish taking the stuff out." I told him he could finish taking the other things out of the boxes in another fifteen minutes. "Now—what kinds of things did you find in the boxes?" I asked. Richie said, "Magazines, newspapers, and toys." Kim said, "Puzzles, crayons, paint and books." Ermine said, "Paper plates, starch, beans, rice and chalk." Albert said, "Popcorn, numbers and things to play music with."

With this list enumerated, I asked the children to name the kind of activities they might carry on in their room. Tommy said, "Art." Suzy said, "Singing songs." Lenore said, "I want to learn to read." Donald said, "I don't know how to write my name." Sandy said, "Play." Cheri said, "Go on field trips."

After the children finished naming the activities they wanted, I suggested they finish taking the things out of the boxes and look around the room for a place to have music, games, art, number games, block games, reading activities and writing. I told them they would again work for fifteen minutes. Tommy said, "We will have to hurry up 'cause fifteen minutes is not long." Again the children were told to report to the rug when they heard the timer ring.

At the end of fifteen minutes, the children sat on the rug to talk for twenty minutes about where activities were to be carried out. Tommy chose a small room for art. He said, "We can use that little room (pointing to another room) to paint because if we spill paint we can clean it up better." Suzy chose another little room for music because the door could be closed and they could make noise with the music things. Lenore chose a corner for reading and a book shelf. Donald chose the center of the room for writing. He said, "We can put a table over there for writing." Sandy said, "We can play in that little room" (pointing to a little room in the far corner of the building).

After the children finished naming places where activities would be conducted, I suggested they start moving the furniture where they wanted it and place the things for each activity in the areas indicated. Someone said, "How long can we have to do that?" I said, "Two fifteen minutes" and everyone went to work.

At the end of the thirty minutes the children gathered on the rug again. Most of the children stated they were tired of working and wanted to play with the toys. I told them they had been working very hard and did a very good job. Then I said, "You can play with the games for one hour."

Each time the children went to work, the Neighborhood Youth workers and I observed. We were interested in seeing how well the children would work together in the semistructured situation.

At the end of the hour the children talked about what had happened on their first morning in school. Every child had something to say. After this discussion, nutrition was served and we cleaned up. This was our first day of minischool operation.

Talking about "what happened" played an important role in Freddi's minischool program. Also, regular observation of children's responses during their activities provided Freddi with information by which further learning experiences could be arranged. According to Freddi, Lenore wanted "to learn to read" and Donald to write his name:

The goal "to perform academically in areas of reading, writing, math and science" was formulated by my students. Some of the children stated they wanted to read, write and learn numbers.

I feel reading should be incorporated in all subject matters. In my minischool, oral language was used to teach reading. Just as a child learns a spoken language in such a way that he can understand and say things he has never said before, he can also learn to read the printed language in such a way that he can recognize words he has never seen before. In the child's earliest years all language is oral. He hears what is said to him. I feel his reading experience should therefore be designed to give meaning to his oral language. The printed symbols of his speech should be used as a bridge into reading. Print, then, becomes his oral language written down. . . . Since reading is closely connected to the child's *oral language and his writing, writing becomes a part of reading activities . . . they supplement and complement one another. A child gains reading powers by writing. He improves his reading by writing.*

I therefore planned activities to teach Lenore to read and Donald to write. However, all the children were allowed to participate in reading and writing activities.

Reading and writing activities occurred daily. An hour was set aside in which the children could discuss a story that had been read aloud to them, the establishment of an ant colony, an experiment in plant growth, or the vegetable soup that they had made after shopping for the ingredients and preparing them. Art activities were a regular followup to each event, and these "enabled the child to gain insight into the fact that his drawings convey meaning to himself and others." Children were encouraged to elaborate upon the ideas that they had represented graphically, and their explanations or ideas were written down to be read back later on.

The thirty pennies that each child was given to buy vegetables for the soup offered opportunities for mathematics lessons as well as providing one of the criteria for decisions about appropriate purchases. A shadow skipping beside a child who was enroute to the store stimulated questions ("How come there are two of me?") that resulted in experimentation with flashlights, leaves, and dolls. Examination of equipment used by a construction crew developed into a study of the tools man uses to aid him in shaping his world. ("Tools can shape carrot sticks as well as apartment houses, churches, and supermarkets! Does the church's shadow look like the shadow of the supermarket? Why are they different shapes?")

Each day brought the children new experiences, new ways of looking at things and of expressing their thoughts about elements common to their lives. Freddi saw opportunity in everything that she and the children did together with the minischool staff. And she saw to it that they did things that would create opportunity for involvement of the children in what she termed "real-life experiences."

Along with many of the other children, Lenore learned to read the words that carried meanings central to their experiences. The youngsters became astute observers and recorders of their own environment (as well as the environments of ants and experimental plants). They were able to classify and to categorize foods as well as objects within the school setting; they theorized about cause-and-effect relationships, including processes of change. Most important, though, the children in Freddi's minischool learned that asking questions is acceptable, and they asked many of them. They also learned that through informal experimentation they were capable of discovering for themselves some useful answers.

Freddi felt that she accomplished her purposes in the Live Oak minischool *because* she used the children's own ideas and interests. The major outcomes that she sought were not as testable as Lenore's word recognition and Donald's ability to write his name. However, this pretern regarded the experience as one in which she became strong and confident—confident that through a classroom program she could strengthen children by developing their autonomy as learners:

I encouraged the children to initiate and choose their own activities. I believe giving the children an opportunity to make choices now will help them feel more confidence in making choices later in life. . . . The learning experiences in my minischool, I believe, helped generate productive thinkers, allowed freedom of experience and expressions, and developed personal satisfaction in learning for each child.

Freddi had faith in children's ability to become independent learners who could assume some immediate responsibility for organizing their own classroom lives, and, therefore, later responsibility for their own destinies. She trusted children to make decisions, and she created an environment in which it was safe for them to test out their ideas. The children rewarded her by confirming her faith in them. They had learned much. And Freddi, who had occasionally suffered despondency at the enormity of the task, learned that single-handedly she was able to initiate a project and to follow it through—an outcome that surprised no one but Freddi herself.

7

The Black School

Cal was black and independent. He was a person of many paradoxes. He called himself a "practical idealist" and a "Utopian." Yet, being a doer, he had "no time to dream." This conflict shaped all his actions. Always involved in a project, Cal was constantly on the go. During the year of the program he was involved in many projects and often moved in directions contrary to those suggested by the coordinator. He was a hard worker and frenetically active. His pace was supercharged whether he was counseling black students about the draft, tutoring minority youngsters, or working as a substitute teacher.

Throughout the year Cal marched to a different drummer. Only he could determine his needs, he felt, and it seemed at times he met only those program expectations that he regarded as expedient. When directly challenged for his nonparticipation or nonattendance in group planned activities, Cal would reply with the following types of responses: "The structured program—the classes, the readings—are teaching me nothing that I do not already know." He would assert that he had *had* a course in group processes and that he had heard "the same stuff" the group was reading. The program, he said, did not take into account where people were when they came in, and "it's been dragging behind" them instead of making them reach: "Nobody—and I mean *nobody*!— can tell me what I need to see and do. Only *I* know that. I've got my own experience and I know what that is and what will be best for me!"

Many times Cal actually felt that the program kept him from achieving his personal objectives. He claimed he had an ulcer that acted up only when he was deflected from his chosen course of action. He had no time nor inclination to reflect. He would say, "I told you. I have to be active. I don't like to just sit and talk. I don't get anything out of it."

Cal schooled himself to manipulate institutions including the one sponsoring the program. In one seminar Cal noted that people could learn from a variety of experiences and apply what they learned toward survival in the schools. He observed that in his draft counseling he was learning a great deal about how to work through a bureaucracy. These things, he felt, were directly translatable to manipulating any institution, including schools. He was learning to use manipulation to accomplish a given end as well as to avoid regulatory power. The effectiveness of this developing skill was evident in his behavior within the program.

Many times during the year Cal's individual choices conflicted with institutional demands. When financial problems beset him, he decided to work as a substitute teacher, although by doing so he was not able to gain the broad point of view about teaching or to develop the continuing relations with children that the program had intended. Rationalizing his behavior to the program director, he said that he could not learn any more by being in someone else's classroom and that what he needed to do was to be on his own. The director agreed that he could substitute one day a week. A week later, Cal reported that he had spoken with people at a local school district and that they were eager to employ him as a full-time substitute for the rest of the school year. "It is that or drop out of the program," he concluded.

Although he was rarely seen on campus, Cal's influence over the potential teacher leaders was substantial. Whether he was present or absent from the group, his actions conveyed a message to his peers: Blackness was an essential criterion for teaching black children. He would join the group at times when he was least expected. On those occasions, however, he was capable of real involvement. He was both gregarious and a loner.

Cal chose to go it alone in his minischool. He had many false starts, since he rarely thought about the consequences of his actions before rashly committing himself. First he decided to take a position in a summer session run by a local school district. He was dissuaded from this course of action by his advisor who reminded him that he would be the victim of those constraints that surround any ongoing program and would not be free, therefore, to make major innovations or to "do his thing."

He then decided to use a recreation center in a small nearby community to set up a school of his own. He had second thoughts, however, when he considered that this school would only be temporary and would have no continuity or permanence. He came to realize that when his enterprise shut down six weeks after it began, the students whom he was serving might be left without continuing influence. The experimental nature of the project also gave him pause. He was against using his people as "guinea pigs" so that he might better himself and earn a degree. He could not see "prostituting black folks."

For too long black folks had been the victims of institutional racism, Cal felt. White society, not individual tyranny, had robbed the black man of his selfhood and identity. It had made him passive and faceless:

The institutions of the United States are supportive of the majority. The historical oppressive relationship which Blacks have experienced from Whites are welded into all of this nation's social institutions. To attack an individual is but foolishly to harbor displaced revenge. In this sated nation, it is the institutions which are shaping man into their docile servant.

So emotional was Cal about this idea that he chose to express these feelings through poetry:

Equality is to me the absurd
To you –, freedom – liberty
and yes – justice
– yet only a word –
You feed upon it until satiety
Knowing its presents, its wonders
yet I hunger for equality

We wonder who might
absorb the knowings
or hasten the pace
of this malevolent race
in so still a night
conjuring faith
in what might prove to them
the root of their malice
in somber pleadings
the willingness of the night
and the briefs to tomorrow's span

Equality of all
in nations many
find they that come
a place of meaning
where life is hope
and death the revival
defined by me
as a place not of sea
or of lands find
but a thought
the suppressor of mind

Even with the changing climate of the sixties, Cal felt it was futile to expect white institutions to remedy the situation. Changes that had been legislated had made only surface differences:

Blacks have demanded that Black Studies courses be added to the curriculum in high schools and colleges. Title I of the Elementary and Secondary Education Act (ESEA) at the elementary level gave extra financial assistance to schools serving students from low economic families. A host of programs have been gorged at each level with monies and energies in an attempt to rectify the deplorable conditions of this country's educational institutions and to appease its minorities. . . . With all these efforts, one might expect to witness massive improvement; but at best, one views a sweet facade of clamoring hope.

Cal felt that for black people to survive, they would have to make their own strides toward equality. One way of doing this was to establish black institutions that would be alternatives to the "white enslaving system":

One can talk of change, but it is meaningless unless institutions are made to serve mankind, not to enslave it. An institution should become an agent for personal esteem, and not an elixir for mass adaptation.

The problems that affected the nation's blacks were tremendous, Cal realized. One of the most pressing was to reverse the "welfare mentality" that plagued so many of his people. The state of mind that encouraged passivity and receiving without giving was self-defeating. It stifled a person's initiative and stagnated the learning process. Cal was certain that blacks must learn to be doers and to establish their own institutions that would be instruments of change. In the past the welfare mentality was essential to black survival. Now, however, it only served to bring about internal alienation and self-defeat. "It is necessary for Blacks to recognize the crippling effects of this welfare mentality and to combat it," he stated. "If not, the present Black struggle may never prove fruitful."

Clearly this participant believed that new institutions were needed. Coincidently, the year before, a black alternative school had been established in a nearby "spiritually depressed" city. Its implicit premise was that it was possible to create a school of quality based solely upon the black experience of conflict with the whites who had exploited them for so long. Apparently assumed also were ideas about the nature of the new black experience in which power relationships might be reversed to the socioeconomic benefit of blacks. Cal was elated to find an existing foundation upon which he could build:

My visions of the potential of the school were unbounded. I had faith in the idealist view that Blackness was the most important criterion for successful operation of an independent Black institution.

Although Cal decided to align himself with the ongoing project, he had been required, like the other preterns, to submit a proposal describing his goals and objectives for the summer, how he was going to achieve them, and how they were to be evaluated. In June he was reminded that his long-delinquent plan of operation was due as was his tentative budget. What he then provided was a mimeographed statement that had been prepared by the Black School staff to be used for fund raising and publicity purposes. When told that this statement was not what had been expected, Cal hastily sketched out a three page overview of his summer plans and promised to hand in "something soon." He explained the delay in submitting a proper proposal by stating that his students really had to participate in the "in-depth plan." "It is important that they are an intricate part in the clarification of the requirements for their school," he said.

Instead of his minischool budget, Cal submitted a statement regarding a Pan-African conference that he wished to attend:

Since most of the expenses of running my minischool will be met by the day school budget, I have a little more freedom to attempt other kinds of things with my allotted funds. There will be three people attending the conference and I would like to have money allotted for registration, living, and gas for these three persons (myself included) for two days in San Diego.

He defended the use of minischool funds for this purpose in terms of staff and community development:

Since the curriculum of my minischool has its main stress upon the relevance of community growth, I feel that it is of utmost importance to have some way of training my staff in the total aspect of community development. The thrust of the Congress of African Peoples is interested in preparing Black people for community involvement. It is a step past that curriculum emphasis of traditional Black Studies (history, culture, etc.). What is needed and what we hope to emphasize in the minischool is active involvement and interpretation of past events. For this reason I deem it necessary to attend this conference as a preparatory.

The director authorized attendance at the conference contingent upon Cal's submission of a report on the proceedings which was to accompany his statement for reimbursement of expenses. This report (a page and a half) appeared the following week; the in-depth plan for his minischool program at the black school never appeared.

The Black School had been founded by a group of black community people and college students. It had been in full-time operation during its first summer when it was able to raise $36,000 from the Teenage Community Action Program. It continued to function on Saturdays during the year with volunteer staffing and whatever money could be raised.

The Black School's second summer program was designed to influence many groups in the community. Primarily it was intended to involve teenagers at a number of different levels. Its overriding purpose was to improve their own academic performance; but its mission was also to give them a sense of pride and accomplishment by involving them in community projects. They met in the mornings from nine to twelve. The curriculum consisted of black history, black literature, and "Blackology" (black psychology). Since these same young people were to spend their afternoons teaching preschool children, there was also some time given to instruction in the strategies of tutoring. The thirty-five teenagers were separated into three classes with eleven to twelve students in each. Pairs of college students were responsible for two of the classes, and Cal was in charge of the third.

In the afternoons, from one to three o'clock, the high school students went into three black neighborhoods of the city. They worked with some sixty young children in the hope of influencing their academic development. Getting the children ready to read was their main thrust. The teenagers, working on porches, in backyards, and in neighborhood parks, were paid to teach the alphabet, colors, correct speech patterns, and "beginning linguistic reading." Cal did not participate directly in this segment of the project although he drove a bus, hauled hot lunches, collected materials, and did whatever he could to support this aspect of the program. The remaining minischool funds were spent on paper and pencils for use by the younger children.

A third thrust involved high school students who did not attend the morning session. They, with one of the staff members, were involved in developing community action projects such as obtaining a sickle cell anemia mobile unit for the area and visiting local supermarkets to survey price differences between black and white neighborhoods. A slide presentation that depicted life in the city was also compiled and was shown to several civic groups.

A fourth part of the program, in which Cal was also involved, was targeted at eight to twelve year olds. Its objective was to increase these children's skills in reading, writing, and mathematics and to explore black history. Six high school girls were assigned to work with Cal.

To the pretern's bitter disappointment, the program did not work out as he had planned. In the mornings there were problems in the three areas of content, form, and student-teacher relations:

In general, the high school program was not very beneficial. A tremendous amount of time was spent trying to solve internal problems. Many of the students looked upon the college teachers in peer fashion and refused to accept any kind of pupil-teacher relationship. When the college staff attempted to assume the role of "teacher" and add the desperately needed leadership, many of the students rebelled, viewing it as though the teachers were "trying to be somethin' they ain't."

Clearly this situation was again a paradox to Cal, for he felt the high schoolers were desperately looking for leadership from the teaching staff but could not accept it. He attributed these interpersonal problems to the fact that the college students had a different and intimate relationship with the younger students outside of school, and since the age differences were minimal, remaining aloof and assuming a more distant role was difficult. "These were the same people with whom we joked and partied many times," Cal stated. From this situation, Cal reported in his final paper, he learned he was "unable to appeal for status and make the relationship work." He discovered that any respect a teacher received had to be a function of his expertise and ability.

While the content of the morning classes differed from that of their establishment counterparts, there were very few differences in organization. Cal lectured for the most part, and the students listened:

We spent about 95 percent of our time in the classroom preaching when we should have been providing opportunities for the students to experience, react, and interpret situations for themselves. . . .

In evaluating outcomes, Cal felt that the summer project too closely followed the framework of the public schools and that the staff did not take full advantage of their independence:

Most of the high school students were unenthusiastic about the Black curriculum, especially since it was presented in a fashion similar to the public school class. However, all the college staff strived for a creativity which was not taken advantage of by the students.

The "teachers" tried to make the classes interesting although their skill was limited. When discussions did occur, Cal clearly did not recognize their value and viewed them as unacademic rap sessions:

Many Black students seem to have the idea that Black Studies is an opportunity to mess around and rap. Or they see it as a time to put down the white man. Even though the students tried to turn everything into rap sessions, a few academic exchanges occurred.

Cal's luck was not much better with the preteenagers with whom he worked in the afternoons. Although he felt that the children enjoyed themselves, only a few educational alternatives were provided. Of most value were two activities that Cal had not planned. First, there had been a kindling of interest in the economic factors that affected the children's lives. This interest led to the design of a flow chart that traced familiar products from production to consumption. Second, using his ability to capitalize upon the events of the moment, Cal permitted the students to play out their emotions through vivid simulations. What evolved was a useful mode of solving the many interpersonal problems that arose in his classroom and a growing awareness that flexibility can be a teacher's most important resource.

Interpersonal problems were not limited to the classroom. Two of his six assistants had severe difficulty in relating to the smaller children. They would sneak into the bathroom to administer drugs to themselves—perhaps to escape the tension. Cal felt strongly that the staff decision to "hush up" the problem and to transfer the older girls away from the younger children was the path of least resistance and that doing so obviated the necessity of coming to grips with the problem.

In what was for him a rare reflective stance, Cal looked back later upon his summer experience and expressed a feeling that he might have used his time, energy, and resources in a different manner:

I failed to take full advantage of what was offered. My prejudices surfaced in a manner which prevented me from truly exploring many of the paradigms. This has crippled me, but not irreparably. It was convenient for me to criticize and refute many of the methods and ideas presented throughout the program, regarding them as inefficient and irrelevant to me as a Black teacher attempting to relate (teach) to Black students. I condemned the academics as being meaningless, where solutions were barrenly conceived. By doing this I failed to allow myself to adapt these ideas to meet my needs. I violated my own laws of survival.

8 La Escuelita

For nearly a century and a quarter a great majority of the American people have not recognized the existence, language, culture, or heritage of more than six million of their fellow Americans: the Chicanos. Because of this lack of recognition of a group that contributed substantially to the growth of the Southwest, these citizens have come to deprecate themselves.

Who am I? Where do I come from? These are important questions to any American child. However, Victor, Flora, and Maria felt that the schools had not helped young Mexican-Americans, especially, to find answers to these questions. In fact, by failing to recognize and accept *chicanidad* as a legitimate factor in the educational process, the schools had contributed to the Chicano's self-doubts. Textbooks and the curriculum had either depicted people of Mexican ancestry in a negative fashion or denied their existence altogether. In the view of the Chicano participants, a people's language, culture, and experiences had been "devalued, ignored . . . and destroyed," and with these their sense of importance and worth.

Not only have Chicanos been looked upon as aliens in their own land, but they have, the preterns felt, suffered "lingual-cultural genocide." Evidence of this was the "English only" Anglo-oriented school systems of the southwestern region of the United States. They saw schools as places where Chicanitos' special way of being human was being taken from them in a destructive process of acculturation into dominant ways and usage of the English language only. The Chicano participants did not think that most teachers would consciously attempt to destroy children, but by denying them their language and culture, they had, indeed, done just that.

The preterns mourned the destruction and eradication of their identity, including their history and their mother tongue. They felt the separation from their roots was a personal tragedy, and they stated that many of these feelings, which were also present in the psyche of their fellow Chicanos, could have been avoided if they had recognized their own worth and the richness and virility of their own Indian-Spanish culture.

The participants learned that the average school years completed by the Chicano population averaged 7.1 as opposed to 9.0 for blacks and 12.1 for Anglos. They attributed these differences to the deprecation of a people's way of being human. Therefore, if schooling were to become a force for positive change and to serve as a vehicle of cultural democracy, new educational processes had to be instituted.

75

Through La Escuelita, Victor, Flora, Mia, and the two Anglo preterns who planned to work with them sought alternatives to the existing educational system. By alternatives, they meant educational experiences that not only enabled Chicanos to participate economically and politically in the dominant society, but also enabled them to determine their own destinies:

The Chicano's self concept is central to the minischool. We hope that la Escuelita will provide an atmosphere where he can develop intellectual and emotional self-confidence. Within our ability each child will be provided with every opportunity and offered every encouragement to recognize his own capabilities. ... He will be given individualized instruction and guidance. He will learn according to his own learning speed and style, if we can determine what those are. The atmosphere will be informal and as full of chicanidad as possible.

The group planned to involve parents and other members of the community in order to make their minischool an active neighborhood force, and to have the residents realize that they can be a part of their children's education. The preterns hoped that parents and teachers could find ways of working together.

As we look forward to la Escuelita we realize that we know less, rather than more, of how to create successful alternatives. Therefore, we hope to maintain an open, flexible, and accepting attitude in order to find alternatives to what we know is happening and to make ourselves more aware of what can occur and more able to effect it. We seek the best for our children because the very best is not good enough.

Their quest for better than "the very best" was a source of considerable tension. However, part of the anxiety that was manifested with regard to La Escuelita may be endemic to the conflict which is inherent in biculturalism. The five participants who planned the minischool tried to straddle two cultures and meld them within a single program. Although mounted upon a strong and bigger indictment of the damage that Anglo programs have inflicted upon Mexican-American children, the minischool proposal written by three Chicano and two Anglo participants outlined six weeks of imaginative, integrated activities. With these activities the planners of the minischool hoped to increase or awaken Chicano identity by:

Providing un ambiente where the Chicanito will have the opportunity to learn and be himself;

Developing a curriculum in language arts and mathematics based upon the personal needs of the Chicano student;

Taking a variety of field trips in an effort to broaden the immediate environment of the students.

Activities for each week of the minischool's operation were designed around a theme. Pre-Columbian Art, Mexican folklore, art, needlework, and cooking were to be central to the program. In the last week, each child was to choose an interest of his own to explore. Consultants, including parents and local artisans who could contribute concretely to the understanding of each theme, were to be invited. Related field trips were planned, and in-school projects tentatively agreed upon.

Developing language skills was a central objective of the curriculum. The planners felt that educational success is based upon learning to speak, read, write, and communicate one's ideas, feelings, and impressions. Because of a lack of appropriate materials available for the Chicano children, the group decided that the Chicanitos would supply their own. Plans were made for the children to tell their own stories in recording studios. These studios, constructed like a rocket ship and a house, which Victor had built and tested in a classroom during the spring, were expected to stimulate childrens' oral language output. Chicanitos would be free to use the language with which they were more comfortable, either Spanish or English. Later the "teachers" would transcribe and duplicate the stories in *both* languages for the children to review the following day. By permitting each child to use the language of preference, the student would be able to "focus upon himself and his own world, not on some abstract ideas often written in a language unfamiliar to him." Listening to reruns of their taped accounts, while reading simultaneously printed versions of their stories, would enable the children to build bridges between the spoken and written word, the preterns felt. Having their own words printed in two languages would help children to gain bilingual reading competence as well.

Through such a program, the group hoped that the children would become interested in books, and would actively seek material to read and enjoy. Even more important, this approach to language development was intended to build self esteem: By preserving the childrens language and their thoughts, each would be respected and the children would gain a sense of worth.

Concurrent with this experiential approach to reading, the preterns planned an elaborate phonics component. They expected the Chicanitos to be able to make sound-symbol associations of vowels and consonants, to attack words phonetically, and, they said, to learn the "thirty-three most common dipthongs in the English language." Sandpaper letters were to offer a multisensory experience with the physical structure of letters; games such as Lotto would be used to develop word attack skills.

Mathematics was included in the curriculum of La Escuelita so that the children might gain confidence working with quantitative relationships. Emphasis on "learning by discovery" was intended to effect long-range achievement:

. . . *This model of teaching is particularly attractive because it appears more conducive to the development of abstract reasoning which is so necessary for successful work at the secondary and college level especially in science and math.*

Art media were to be utilized as means of expressing the chosen themes. Once a week the children were to get a chance to share their paintings, sculpture, murals, puppets, and so forth. They could use either English or Spanish as a vehicle for communication with their peers. Each child might choose and speak in the language of comfort.

The group felt that the most pressing deficiency in teachers presently working with Mexican-American children was their almost universal inability to communicate in Spanish. This deficiency contributed to the destruction of a person's humanness by denying him his mother tongue, the key to his cultural heritage. If this were the only cause for what they termed "cold alienation," Anglo teachers might be trained to work with Spanish-speaking people. The problem, however, was regarded as more complex: To be effective, teachers must internalize the personality and culture of their students. They also must be aware of the nuances of differences among Chicano children. The preterns believed that factors like ruralism, urbanism, date of immigrancy, degree of assimilation, and political-philosophical orientation all contributed to different outlooks and learning styles.

Clearly, the three Chicanos felt that by virtue of their heritage, they were well equipped to deal with Mexican-American children:

It must be remembered that we, Victór, Flora, and Mia, came to the program committed to the idea of the advancement of the Chicano. All three of us have been involved in Chicano community action groups committed to the concept of self determination of the Chicano community. Because of our suppressed, discriminatory treatment by Anglo dominated institutions, Chicanos believe that the self-determination of our community is now the only acceptable mandate for social and political action; it is the essence of the Chicano commitment.

The preterns saw Chicano teachers as essential because of their modeling capability. When speaking Spanish and presenting the Mexican culture and heritage in a positive manner, such teachers would provide models with which a Chicano child could identify.

As a minischool group, Mia, Flora, and Victor came together naturally. Their friendship had developed because they were the only Chicanos in the program. They were able to talk and confide in each other since they had common life experiences that bound them together. They felt a responsibility to see that "La Raza and Chicanoism were represented and given proper exposure."[a] Also, aside from cultural-philosophical commonalities, the three were the only married preterns in the program. Their commitments and obligations contrasted greatly with those of the single participants.

---

[a]Literally meaning "The Race," *La Raza* is a term which rallies the emotions of the Chicano around the shared history and culture of a people.

Sylvia, a fourth pretern, participated in La Escuelita on a part-time basis.[b] She was involved in the planning and then left the area for a time. Physical problems prevented her from full participation. A statement by the three Chicanos reflected a respect for Sylvia's skills, but also their hesitation to embrace her as an equal member in a project that they felt required ethnic expertise and was a Chicano response to Anglo domination:

As a member of a distinct ethnic minority group, Sylvia is extremely sensitive to the feelings and needs of others. She is an intelligent person with a healthy outlook on cultural democratization. Sylvia never made presumptuous statements about what people outside of her immediate reality and experience needed. Not being a Chicano, Sylvia felt that she could never fully know nor understand a culture so outside her "real world." Instead, Sylvia kept an open mind and never made major philosophical statements about bilingualism, biculturalism, or Chicanoism.

Implied in the tribute was the suggestion that other nonChicanos associated with the Teacher Leader Program had made such statements.

The preterns were aware that the success of La Escuelita would be dependent upon extensive planning and field work. Having spent many months reading about and observing experimental programs, they were alert to the necessity of a carefully organized project. They had seen too many attempts at innovation that did not function as originally proposed, and they were adamant about not having their program become an unsuccessful "experiment." Victor considered what he described as the Anglo proclivity to experiment on Chicano children as much a reason for the children's failure to achieve by Anglo standards as the inappropriateness of the programs offered them. "Chicanos are not guinea pigs!" he often stated.

Before their field explorations began, Victor and the others met weekly for three months to work out the details for La Escuelita. Final plans had to depend, however, on the site selected for the school. Many nearby communities were examined. They ranged from urban to rural, from new housing developments to old barrios. The group collected literature and contacted community leaders. They finally considered two areas. One was part of a large city and the other in a smaller one. Even though people with whom they spoke in both areas were receptive to the group's proposal, the large city site was chosen because a stronger base of Chicano support was evident in the area.

The group arranged meetings with school people: the principal of a neighborhood school, the school's Title I coordinator, a community-school liason staff worker. These school persons, all Chicanos, were most supportive. The

---

[b] A fifth pretern was influential in planning the minischool with the others. This pretern left the program in June in order to teach school in a small Mexican village.

preterns were allowed to visit many of the bilingual and ESL (English-as-a-Second-Language) programs already existing in the school district. They felt that becoming familiar with what was going on within the establishment was important so that they could know the reality of the children's previous educational experience.

Many other contacts were made, including those with a leading community organizer in the area and the chairman of the local Mexican-American Political Association (MAPA). The group also attended several meetings that included planning sessions for a community bicultural organization that was being developed. From these, the preterns gained insight into the wishes of the community regarding the education of its children. Concomitantly, the community became aware of plans being made for the summer project. The neighborhood the preterns decided upon had a total—adult and child—Chicano population of 18 percent. The community school was 48 percent Mexican-American; black students comprised 37 percent, and Anglos 14 percent of the student body. The socioeconomic level of most families was low, which thus qualified the school's program for federal poverty funding.

The search for an adequate site for the minischool was extensive. After the decision to remain close to the area surrounding the elementary school had been made, the group contacted three realtors in the vicinity and explained their needs. Several houses, a community theater, and a vacant school were investigated. Only the vacant school was available for summer rental, but careful inspection revealed that it was too run down to be considered.

After a great deal of thought, the preterns rejected the idea of a "nonschool associated facility." They felt a "storefront" school would not benefit the greatest number of children because most of them lived in single-family dwellings far from a business district. In the east, where the storefront concept originated, population density is greater and shopping areas more available. Thus, the preterns believed that ". . . the neighborhood public school plant would be ideal if we could be given reasonable freedom in running our school." Additionally, after talking to many Mexican-American parents and observing their relationship to the public schools, the group had come to feel that neighborhood families would be more receptive to having their children attend a summer school sanctioned by "the establishment" than one whose purposes were not given the credibility of such recognition.

Another factor in the preterns' decision was their conviction that children learn best in a familiar environment where they feel secure and safe. The school would provide a physical setting for their program that was not alien to the children, as it was a part of their neighborhood life. Also, the preterns reasoned that in a little school associated with the public school environment, Chicanitos' feelings about La Escuelita would carry over to the regular school program and they would "gain a positive concept of the whole school experience." Victor, Mia, Flora, and Sylvia were concerned about this factor—that is, the minischool's having a continuing impact on the educational experience of the children.

The school's principal, also a Mexican-American, reacted enthusiastically to a proposal to use his facilities. He helped the preterns contact administrators at school district headquarters, as well as representatives of the Department of Parks and Recreation. After a meeting with several officials and a presentation of the plan to the Board of Education, the project was approved.

Then the group began to narrow its perspective. From the broad goals they had formulated, they discussed and selected specific ones:

Encourage spontaneity and self-motivation;

Familiarize the children with the phonetic sounds of the English language;

Reinforce reading skills;

Encourage children to express their thoughts and feelings in Spanish and English;

Encourage emotional involvement in mathematical activities;

Emphasize understanding and discovery rather than rote learning of math techniques;

Provide children with the kinds of stimulation necessary for their creative growth;

Facilitate creativity in a maximum variety of ways such as cutting, pasting, use of color, mixing colors, use of form, use of various media;

Help children initiate a project and determine materials and techniques to accomplish an end;

Encourage discovery of creative uses for materials commonly found in the environment;

Stimulate and enhance the growth of self-concept *para que el joven estime y sienta orgullo de su cultura y de su ser y no le tenga o le sienta vergüenza a nada y a nadie* [so the young person may feel good about himself and feel pride in his culture and in his being and so that he does not feel ashamed in relation to anyone about anything].

"Chicanidad," they stated, "will permeate all activities and the children will feel free to be themselves." They designed their program to make ethnic identity (including the Spanish language) a positive force. At the same time, they sought to strengthen the English language skills and other competencies necessary to self-determination in a technological society.

Armed with these dual purposes, the group met with staff members at the school and explained their project. They asked the teachers to suggest Chicano students who were having academic difficulties and who, they felt, would most benefit from La Escuelita.

The group talked with about sixty children over the next few weeks, explaining the general program to them both in Spanish and in English. They sent "registration" forms home to parents along with a description of La Escuelita. About thirty of the forms were returned and the preterns began scheduling conferences with parents at their homes. The talks were time consuming but fruitful:

We spent an average of thirty to forty minutes at each home explaining our school and encouraging their participation in la Escuelita. We feel these home visits were not only valuable in enlisting the support of the parents, but also had a great deal to do with the good attendance we had at the school. We were received warmly in each home and found no rejection of our project.

The preterns tried to communicate to parents a hope that they would play an active role in the summer project:

We plan to involve parents and other members of the community in order that la Escuelita can become a part of the community, and to have the community realize that they can and must be part of their children's education. This will allow parents and teachers to work together.

Out of the forty-two homes visited, the group registered thirty-three students. The other nine students did not participate because summer plans conflicted with minischool sessions.

The two weeks before La Escuelita was to open its doors were spent in final preparations. The preterns organized the room, arranged field trips, and secured consultant help. The group hired a teacher aide, a young Chicana, who was paid a salary of one hundred dollars for the six weeks of work. She assisted in teaching, helped prepare the midmorning snack, and assumed many housekeeping duties.

Victor was designated as "director" of the school by the three other preterns. First by tacit understanding and later by acclamation, he was *el jefe,* the leader. His responsibility was to be the school's public relations representative. Each of the other preterns also had specific areas of responsibility. These included maintaining the budget, purchasing food and camera supplies, ordering and obtaining library films, handling written communication, and purchasing educational supplies. As the moment of truth approached, the Chicano participants experienced considerable anxiety because their ego involvement in the project went beyond that of personal identity.

Since they had identified La Escuelita as a school for Chicanos, Flora, Maria, and Victor had a dual investment in its outcome: (1) its success—and similarly its failure—would be that of Chicano teachers; (2) its children were *their* children, and on the children's future depended the future of La Raza. One participant's withdrawal from the program and Sylvia's partial involvement, served to intensify the Chicanos' burden of responsibility and its resultant tension. Because of this tension they had second thoughts about their planned exploration into the cultural roots of the expressive arts.

The proposed program, which had looked excellent on paper a month before, stood as a threat to the three Chicanos. In it they had given substantial recognition to the importance of "basic skills" in the enhancement of their children's self-concepts. These were to be developed indirectly through culturally relevant activities. However, the group could not shed their sense of urgency about teaching basic skills. They viewed literacy and computational skills as important instruments for competitive achievement. They saw such achievement as essentially related to self-determination in the "real" (i.e., Anglo) world.

Though they *knew* "traditional" classroom methods had generally failed with Chicano children, their own experience within the system (while it had cost them dearly) had been one of relative success. One of the prices they had paid had been hard work. It was difficult for the Chicanos to believe that really important learning—learning that pays off in achievement—could be fun. Besides their dual purposes, they suffered conflict regarding the means by which their goals were to be achieved.

Without the support of the Anglo participants with whom they had drawn up their proposal, the Chicano preterns who launched the program established its parameters within the safety of the known. They built a fairly traditional program within a traditional classroom setting. They erected it upon a pro-Chicano, anti-Anglo stance of trying to beat the Anglo at his own game. Besides an attack on "the fundamentals," their strategies included employing Mexican artifacts, playing Mexican music, and capitalizing upon the teachers' ethnic identity with the children through charismatic use of the Spanish language and through direct exercise of paternalistic authority. Although these teacher behaviors may have been justifiable in terms of culture-matching teaching strategies, they militated against some stated objectives—that is, developing an easy interaction between the minischool and the Mexican-American community. Some of their approaches to the vaunted "fundamentals" also failed to promote a number of other objectives, such as "to encourage spontaneity and self-motivation" and "to emphasize understandings and discovery rather than rote learning."

In their quest for certainty and to protect themselves from any suggestion that their program was not exemplary, the Chicano staff of La Escuelita tended to reject all things "Anglo," while they inconsistently embraced many activities and experiences—for example, taking the little Chicanos to an art musuem to see Gainsborough's "Blue Boy"—because "that's what the middle-class parents of achieving Anglo children do."

Sylvia's return at the end of the second week signaled a return to a less constricted perspective. She was a trusted and outspoken member of the team.

Since Sylvia had a genuine respect for her colleagues and what they hoped to do, the Chicanos were willing to review their initial actions in the light of her perceptions. They began to see some of their teaching behaviors and activities as counterproductive. Having assured themselves that they could establish and manage a program without external support, the Chicano preterns were able to work *with* this Anglo pretern in a climate of mutual trust and support despite conflicts regarding philosophy, approaches to teaching-learning, and stylistic differences.

The classroom in which the four preterns taught together was a bungalow on the grounds of the chosen elementary school. The room measured approximately twenty by thirty feet. However, the facility that the school district provided at no charge had no running water and no cooling system, which are distinct disadvantages in a hot Southern California valley. In an attempt to "invest the room with a sense of culture," the preterns decorated its walls with posters, banners, and symbols of the contemporary Chicano movement. Stenciled reproductions of Mexican designs, more archeological than political in origin, were also displayed. Bulletin boards and posters carried legends in both Spanish and English. Pictures of Mexican and Chicano heroes predominated, but Indian folk art was also evident. In a place of honor on the back wall, a picture of each child was displayed. These were taken the first day of school to give each student a sense of importance and worth.

The spatial arrangement of the room was flexible and the furniture could be moved to accommodate the current activity:

We had tables, chairs, and bookcases available in the classroom and we added a four-by-six-foot playhouse, and a three-by-eight-foot high rocket for the children to use. We also brought orange crates into the classroom. These crates were used as lockers for the students with each student having his name attached to his own locker. The lockers were used to store all the materials assigned to the students and also for any personal belongings they wished to place in them.

The first week a class of twenty-seven students attended; the second week the enrollment dropped to twenty-four where it remained all summer. Attendance averaged about twenty. Many of the children were absent because they went to visit relatives in Mexico for a time, a practice that reflects the close ties remaining between many Mexican-Americans and their ancestral roots.

Students in La Escuelita ranged from five to ten years of age. For most, Spanish was the native tongue, but competency in both English and Spanish varied widely. In the classroom, one could hear both languages at any time.

The school operated for six weeks, five days a week from the middle of June to the last of July. Children attended from nine o'clock until noon, although on several occasions field trips lasted all day. At least two of the staff opened the room at eight in the morning to encourage the children to come early if they wished. Consequently, the children began arriving at eight and continued, a few at a time. The preterns consciously decided not to scold the children who were late, a practice employed during the regular school year and often demeaning to these youngsters. Originally, time segments were not allotted, but the preterns came to feel that math and language activities should be pursued each day and a "daily schedule" resulted.

The children's spontaneous enthusiasm for games led the preterns to make this unplanned activity a part of the daily program each morning from eight to nine. Games, including spelling and phonic card games, were bought with project funds; there were games for learning to tell time and for learning arithmetic "facts"; there were counting beads, building blocks, and checkers. Playing games with the children on a one-to-one basis, the participants realized, not only provided opportunities for skill development but "an opportunity for our Chicanitos to develop a close relationship with a Chicano teacher."

Flora, Mia, and Victor felt that such a relationship was essential to the development of communication skills and therefore the preterns joined in the play, upon invitation. By contrast, the succeeding period of time was formal and ritualistic, with "Opening Exercises" and the taking of the roll. Attention then turned to mathematics and the language arts. The last hour of the morning, after recess and a snack, was reserved for art and films.

The preterns, despite the schedule, reserved the right to make ad hoc decisions:

Some days games or art took the whole morning, whereas others consisted mainly of writing or reading stories. When the weather was very warm, we took cold watermelon or ice cream across the street to a small park and spent an hour or so just talking, playing, and enjoying each other's company.

As the minischool teachers worked with the children, instruction came to be based on grouping by language dominance, in Spanish and English. Three groups emerged consisting of those who were primarily Spanish speaking, those who were more competent in English (most of whom understood Spanish), and those for whom dominance could not be determined:

We felt that even though our program was geared toward individualized instruction, we wanted to carry out this individualization within small groups. In other words, lessons were prepared in either Spanish, or English, or a combination of both languages according to the needs of the particular group. Following the presentation, the children were then worked with individually. Consequently, even though Spanish and English was used in the classroom at all times, the actual presentation of a specific lesson was usually done in the above manner. It should also be pointed out that this method was useful because it helped to save time during a presentation by using only one mode of communication.

Therefore, the purpose of grouping was to enable us to present material to the children in the language that was most familiar to them, and also to utilize our time as teachers to the utmost.

La Escuelita's teachers screened the children's language abilities informally. During the first few days of their program, they made a point of speaking to all the children in both languages. Notes were kept and observations were shared. Tentative assignments were made, but in some cases the preterns' initial opinion was not found to be valid and a child was assigned to another instructional group.

Victor worked with the Spanish-speaking children. He used Spanish for directions and explanations; children were encouraged to reply in Spanish in order to become confident in their oral expression. Although English was recognized as an alternate language, it was used sparingly.

Mia used both tongues interchangeably. However, children were encouraged to dictate or write their stories in English since that was the language they needed for success in school.

Flora emphasized oral language patterns in English. The children kept diaries and could share their writing with other members of their group. However, Flora often spoke to her charges in Spanish "for identity purposes."

At La Escuelita, communication skills were given the highest priority:

For the Chicanito, success in this area has often been minimal due to the linguistic and cultural differences encountered at the school. In most schools, teachers are culturally deficient, and language arts materials suitable for the instruction of Chicano students are lacking. In addition, current reading materials used in the schools today offer very little with which the Chicano child can relate. California reading texts do not include Spanish-speaking native-born children in their stories. Bilingual children are usually foreigners in a story, thus leaving nothing with which they can identify. The whole heritage of the Chicano child in the Southwest has been completely neglected.

To build their communication skills the children were encouraged to listen, to speak, and to write. The recording booths proved inviting. In them, children recorded their thoughts privately, free from interference by peers and teachers. According to plan, the narrations were transcribed and returned to the students, usually the following day. The reading of these stories was joyful for they were the children's own products and reflected their interests and feelings. Library books were also available and stories about Caesar Chavez and pre-Colombian mythology were read to the children. However, the children's own writings made up somewhat for the dearth of suitable published reading material available to the young Chicano.

The three also assessed children's competence in areas other than language. The preterns constructed a simple diagnostic test to determine computational skill levels. Standardized tests were looked upon with suspicion, since these had been developed by Anglos and their validity for Chicanitos was believed questionable. Following the testing, objectives were established for each child and strategies laid for achieving them. The preterns often reviewed basic mathematics concepts in Spanish, and since the group was multi-aged, the level of difficulty of the exercises varied greatly. Many manipulanda were used, including beads, nuts, drinking straws, and construction paper. These were employed to clarify spatial relationships and numerical operations.

The creative arts were encouraged not only to promote individual expression but also to help achieve a positive identity by stressing cultural themes. Visits by a Chicano artist did a great deal to create enthusiasm:

Mr. Armando showed the children Mexican clay figurines. After his presentation, he demonstrated how to make the figurines. We then broke up into small groups and the children proceeded to make hands, kneeling women, faces, food, burros, birds, babies and a rolling pin in clay. Mr. Armando's ability to communicate in Spanish, his easy, accepting manner with the children and his artistic talents certainly contributed greatly in making la Escuelita's creative arts program a success.

Field trips played an important part in the curriculum of La Escuelita. They provided a rich fund of experience to be used in language arts activities, including reading. Additionally, the preterns felt strongly that all children should have "common experiences" in order to feel confident in an elementary school and part of the mainstream. In talking with parents they found that almost 90 percent of the children had never been to those places that many Southern Californians visit as a matter of course:

Since our students were low-income Chicanitos, they lacked experiences such as visits to the educational centers or amusement sites in the greater Los Angeles area. Low-income families have little money available to spend on recreational and educational activities. Consequently we decided that field trips would be an integral part of our curricular activities. In this way we hoped to avoid having our Chicanitos feel "deprived" or left out because of a lack of common experiences shared by a majority of their peers.

Trips were planned to local places of interest, historical sites, and nationally known tourist attractions. The first outing was to a nearby park that many of the children had never visited. The children enjoyed playing with one another in a new setting, and the experience served to give the preterns knowledge about what to expect from the children on longer, more elaborate ventures.

The second excursion was to a restoration of a Mexican pueblo founded by the Spanish padres. Because of its commercial emphasis, the preterns were dubious of its actual cultural value:

Nothing in the area was noncommercial, but we decided to take this trip and use the experience to accentuate the positive and point out what was obviously stereotypical. . . . We decided that eating in a restaurant would be a good experience for the children, because most of the children had never had the experience of eating in a restaurant. It was marvelous because the children, although very excited, behaved beautifully. The children looked at the menu and debated between hamburgers and tacos. Hamburgers won out! It was hamburgers with french fries for most of the children.

The children later visited a historic mission that had familiar characteristics. Their own churches and the films they had seen at school in preparation for the trip made them feel comfortable and at home. Art work and stories reflected this outing for many weeks.

A visit to the Mexican Ballet Folklorico reinforced the theme of positive cultural identity. The music and dancing were intoxicating to the children who were reluctant to return to the bus they shared with other minischool groups.

A trip to one amusement park was so stimulating that the preterns decided an excursion to Disneyland would be one that the children would remember and treasure, especially since few of the children had been there. When they arrived, a book of ten amusement rides was purchased for each child; each was given an envelope with two dollars to spend as he or she deemed fit. The children bought ice cream, soft drinks, and popcorn as they set out in small groups to explore unimagined wonders. They marvelled at the haunted house, rode the monorail many times, were thrilled by the Pirates of the Caribbean, and enchanted by The Small World. Each group chose a different restaurant to visit for lunch.

For their final outing, on the last day of La Escuelita, the preterns arranged for the children to visit the Lopez Panaderia, a Mexican-American bakery in a nearby town. The Lopez family proudly offered a tour and an explanation in Spanish of the baker's functions. La Señora Lopez identified the many kinds of *pan dulce* being prepared for sale. The huge rotating oven and the mixing vats fascinated the children. And although the breads for the day had already been baked the previous night, small samples of dough had been saved to show the children the different types and textures. The children gained an appreciation for how much skill and work was involved in making the sweet bread so familiar to them and felt the baked *pan dulce* that was waiting tasted twice as good as usual.

Parents, too, appreciated the experiences the minischool offered the children. After La Escuelita closed its doors for the last time, several parents of the children who participated were interviewed. The adults said they were happy that their children had been a part of the school and expressed gratitude that *"los profesores"* had taken their children to so many wonderful places. The parents, the group reported, were pleased that the minischool had given their children an opportunity and the motivation to attend summer school.

In reviewing the summer experience, the preterns felt that their decision to reject the storefront concept and locate at a regular public school site had been justified, although the bungalow, without running water or air conditioning, had been inadequate. Attendance was good, parents felt secure, the students appeared happy and enthusiastic. In addition, the regular administrative staff had not proved to be an impediment to a free and independent project:

Perhaps the overall positive feeling we had at the school was due to the fact that Mr. Garcia, the principal, was totally receptive to our program and demonstrated a great deal of confidence and enthusiasm for it. In other words, he did not require us to submit a formal plan of operation or have us clear each field trip with him. We shared a common bond of dedication to Chicano children and therefore we had mutual trust in each other.

The tone of La Escuelita had been exciting, the preterns reported. The children were "cooperative and "receptive." There were no fights or accidents of any kind:

During the entire duration of la Escuelita we didn't have one behavioral problem. . . . The children were respectful of each other and they were responsible about putting materials in their proper places. All of the classroom rules were self-enforced.

This situation left the preterns free to concentrate on reinforcing the positive behavior and attitudes that led to a "pleasant, cooperative learning environment."

Through the use of both Spanish and English in the classroom, many children who had at first reacted negatively to speaking Spanish in the school setting began to accept this as a more comfortable situation and to express themselves easily and fluently:

When la Escuelita first began, Lupe pretended not to understand or speak Spanish. She went so far as to even deny her Mexicanness. By the second week Lupe began to acknowledge her ability to understand and speak. Later she said she had been born in Mexico and had come to the United States when she was five years old.

The bilingual approach was instrumental, the minischool founders asserted, in leading to the children's more positive self-concepts. Accepting the children's feelings and stressing cooperation and achievement for the family (a positive cultural value) also contributed to achieving this primary objective. Indeed, they felt the classroom became an extended family, a more comfortable arrangement than the usual aloof, Anglo organization.

Perhaps the most rewarding and beneficial aspect of la Escuelita, was the familial feeling which eminated from the group. Four of the regularly enrolled students felt comfortable enough in la Escuelita to bring younger brothers and sisters to our classes.

The group's interpersonal style seemed to contribute more to the project's success than some of the planned "academic" activities. The "communication through authorship" idea, for which the preterns had held high hopes, did not seem to be as effective as expected. At first children did not participate in recording their ideas and feelings but toward the end of the six weeks, more students spontaneously visited the recording booths. Many showed enormous pride when their typed stories were returned to be read aloud to the class. If the summer had been longer, these procedures might have been even more productive. The first results hinted at the direction in which the children were growing:

. . . My name is Paulo, I go to the church with Monica. I see birds, I see water, I see kitchen and I see church and I see santos, and I see white bathrooms and I go home. No more!

. . . I am in love with the music. I don't know what I do with it. At home I just been playing it, hearing it, I don't do nothing else, but do it. But I want Julia to say a story right now. I gotta tape a song here goes. [Song]: You heard my song and that's the end. My teacher teach me that song. And that was my story. And he wanted for me to learn some more and more and every day I did want to.

. . . My name is Dolores. Once I had a dog at Mexico and they ranned over him. The second dog we had they took him to the dog pound. And we had another one and they killed him and then another one and then they took him to the dog pound. Now we don't have any dogs at all not even a cat, at least. Now you've heard my story. Now we don't have any dogs at all . . . and not even a pet at home . . . him die again. Amen. This is my story.

. . . Ayer fuimos a la misión San Gabriel. Salimos de la Escuelita a las nueve de la mañana y llegamos allá a las nueva y trienta. Cuando llegamos a la misión pagamos y compramos los boletos. Después salimos para afuera donde tienen una fuente y tambien vienen las palomas a tomar agua y a comer. Compramos grano para dar le de comer a las palomas. Después pasamos a ver el cañón y las

*casitas. Los hoyos donde hacían jabón, velas y curaban la vaqueta estaban
hondos y las casuelas y metates en la cocina están muy viejas.*
[Yesterday we went to the San Gabriel Mission. We left La Escuelita at nine
o'clock in the morning and arrived there at nine-thirty. When we arrived at the
Mission, we paid for and bought tickets. After that we left to go outside where
they had a fountain and also pigeons came to drink water and to eat. We bought
birdseed to feed the pigeons. Afterwards we went to see the cannon and the
little houses. The holes where they made soap, candles and tanned the hides
were deep and the casserole dishes and corn grinders in the kitchen are very
old.]

In evaluating their curriculum, the preterns felt that many of the children
had made heartening progress in mathematics, too. They attributed achievement
to the opportunity that their program provided for the children to have the concepts explained to them in Spanish. Spanish permeated all of the curriculum:
music, art, and social studies.

After the summer, the group met to evaluate their program. They felt
strongly that others should be able to profit from their experience. Several
suggestions were offered and placed on record as a result of this critiquing
session:

1. Concentrate on only two areas of curriculum at one time;
2. Provide breakfast for the children;
3. Bring in more Chicano adults as role models;
4. Teach Spanish-speaking children to read in Spanish first;
5. Do not attempt a formalized testing program;
6. Use educational games as an integral part of the program;
7. Take many field trips;
8. From the beginning, plan the program with parents;
9. Make the group multi-aged;
10. Have a pleasant physical environment.

The group also felt strongly that the homogeneous nature of the class contributed to the children's satisfaction and achievement. They reasoned that a
mixed cultural group "would have complicated and weakened our major thrust
of enhancing positive Chicano self-identity."

Finally, the prospective teachers felt that their experience with La Escuelita
had helped them to grow professionally: "It provided us an opportunity to
implement techniques in teaching that we might not have been able to carry out
in a typical teaching situation." They had tried to create a situation in which
children they felt very close to could be given "the best of two worlds." But
they recognized that whether these children would "make it" in the Anglo world
and still remain with their own people would depend upon a great deal more
than one six-week program. They wanted to believe that they had helped.

9 Las Palmas

The vitality that characterized the Las Palmas minischool carried no hint of the pain and anxiety that accompanied its birth. The minischool's creators were beset with many difficulties, the most troublesome being that of justifying their own relationship to their offspring project. Boyd, Gail, and Tina sought to do this by affirmatively stating a hypothesis about which in reality they had nagging doubt: "We hypothesized that three white-Anglo adults can create an environment in which minority children are able to learn." They were realistic enough to realize, however, that "only experience would help us formulate our role . . . within an ethnically different setting."

The project the three designed was based upon assumptions that were heartily debated and rejected by most of the minorities among their peers. For this reason and because of other influences, the trio not only questioned the roles appropriate to them in minority-dominated communities, they began to question their own motives as well.

These doubts entered a door set ajar during their early experiences in the program when the entire participant group toured school and community service centers in ethnic minority areas of Los Angeles. With Gail's and Tina's involvement in a course dealing with black identity taught by a psychologist who was a militant spokesman for black separatism, it gained yet a firmer footing on their threshhold of awareness. As the year progressed and they worked with black master teachers in an ethnically mixed neighborhood, the door to questions swung wide, and they agonized over the issue of the white teacher in a minority setting.

The three recognized ambivalence in their own responses to these experiences. They had felt the need for exposure to people from different ethnic backgrounds if they were to deal effectively with minority group members as individuals; such exposure was anathemic to them, however, because it defined them as "visitors" and "observers." They rejected the usefulness of group generalizations in working with individuals; yet the very concept of a "white role" implied the appropriateness of formulating such generalizations. The fact gradually became apparent that if the process were to begin, then self-examination was required:

I am alive to the tremendous problems of subcultures and of cross-cultural communication, to the informal values that exist at an unarticulated, subconscious level. Yet, how can I understand another culture when I can't make generalizations about the dominant group of which I am a member?

93

Boyd, with Tina and Gail, noted that the strength and commitment of minority people dealing with their own problems arose from experiences that were inaccessible to them as members of the dominant group. Following a visit to a mental health center in south central Los Angeles, they lunched in a Black Muslim restaurant, and the three later reflected upon the evidence of ethnic pride they had seen: "The fact that they [blacks] had come to this pride by harnessing their deep-seated rage and preaching against whites gave us much to think about in terms of *our* roles."

The preterns noted that their behavior during cross-cultural contacts was passive and submissive:

Although we were interested in what these people had to say, we rarely posed questions. We feared that our ignorance would be revealed, that we would be labeled white missionaries, that our questions, based on our own preconceptions, might structure the information these people could offer in terms of our generalizations.

In contrast, Tina, Boyd, and Gail observed that they behaved aggressively in situations in which whites were in control of poverty area institutions. Projecting their own uncertainties onto other representatives of the dominant culture, the manner of the preterns was obsessively intense and belligerent. Each seemed to hope that someone like themselves could articulate a solution to their dilemma. While none discovered solutions, each of the three did discover that his or her personal concerns were shared by fellow white, Anglo preterns.

Tina and Gail, especially, came to recognize the sources of energy that inflamed the black separatists. In a context of cultural pluralism, they accepted and respected the belief system expressed. In a theoretical sense, they agreed with the view that "minority people should join together in solving their mutual problems while white people should deal with racism in their own people." However, given the realities of power politics, they questioned the feasibility of minority-controlled schools; and given the communication problems that quite clearly resulted from diverse life experiences, they questioned the desirability of further isolating social groups from one another.

As the issue became highlighted, Gail and Tina sought to resolve the conflict by undergoing a period of intensive classroom participation with two black teachers in a school with a predominantly black student body. What they found there only exacerbated the problem for them. They saw an administration and staff indifferent to the two teachers' efforts to develop ethnic awareness and pride. They saw destructive white substitute teachers who communicated negative expectations and found them fulfilled. But, while the black teachers commanded the respect and love of the children, the teaching appeared to be both uninspired and unproductive. Yet, the fact was evident to them that in spite of educative shortcomings, in these two classrooms children were receiving

". . . positive emotional experiences by subtle means that were not clear to us." Gail and Tina could only conclude:

. . . the emotional security provided the children by a teacher of the same culture was a vital and important aspect. We also felt that if these children were going to succeed they needed skillful teachers who had given more careful consideration to the learning process.

During the second semester course dealing with organizational change, the issue was confronted head-on. As was clear from the start, the discussion was focused generally on the role of the program participants as educational change agents and specifically on the question of whether white Anglos could teach in ethnically different neighborhoods. With her emotional involvement in this problem already heavily invested in a public school practicum and the activities of Black History Week, Tina reacted strongly to the planned course emphasis and chose to do independent study in child psychology instead. However, the concerns of the course and the thinking it stimulated affected *all* of the program participants, especially the white, Anglo preterns for whom its topic of inquiry had become a major preoccupation.

The divisiveness that had subtly characterized the entire program group was given a new meaning and was conceptualized as a cultural reality. Initially, Tina, Gail, and Boyd each had planned to deal with this reality by working cooperatively with a minority pretern in the development and implementation of a minischool program. What these plans signified and how they were altered in time are best indicated by their own words written retrospectively:

This is direct evidence of our uncertainty about the role of an Anglo teacher in a minority community. We did not presume to know what that role involved. We preferred an observing "visitor" status once again. Those plans never materialized, partly because of practical problems. While it is difficult to analyze our own motives, perhaps there was a more important reason: although we each first considered legitimizing our presence in a minority community by working with a minority person, our need to resolve the issue forced us into an alliance based on our cultural sameness. To work with minority interns would have meant more exposure to the "issue" rather than its resolution. The only way to resolve the issue for us was to do it ourselves [emphasis supplied].

For Boyd, Tina, and Gail the minischool they developed was a do-it-yourself project that was also a test. Las Palmas was a test of an idea, and it was a test of themselves. For a while, however, the trio found themselves being tested in ways they had not anticipated.

They discovered an area in which funds for a recreational program at a federal housing project had been depleted. After determining that the children in this project, who were mostly of Mexican descent, had need of a summer program, the three attempted to work through established structures in order to secure the cooperation and the blessing of existing agencies. What they encountered was a politically turbulent community in which cooperation by one faction was resented by another. Petty jealousies and jurisdictional disputes were difficult for the students to deal with. Each attempt on their part to seek solutions seemed to uncover more problems than answers. Additionally, the responsibility for seeking solutions and for mobilizing resources for the opening of the minischool was left in Boyd's hands at the end of the spring semester when both women had to fly east temporarily. Unexpected surgery delayed Tina's return until the minischool program was underway.

The trio ultimately obtained permission to operate their minischool in several rooms of the housing project's community center on the days when the facility was not in use for health clinics and other functions. This arrangement meant that they had to plan off-site activities for the days when the building was not available to them. This problem was alleviated and planning made easier when Gail, Tina, and Boyd rented a mountain home for the summer. In a communal living arrangement, they were able to effectively coordinate their roles and functions. Additionally, the canyon in which they lived offered a rich learning environment to which the children could be transported when the community house was preempted for other activities.

During the planning phase in the late spring, Boyd, Gail, and Tina sought advice, not from Chicano peers or from the Mexican-Americans whose consultive services were available to them, but instead, an American of Oriental descent whose progressive beliefs about teaching and learning were congruent with the assumptions upon which they based their program. Clearly, they were not ignoring the problems of cross-cultural teaching and learning being articulated in their cultural anthropology course, but rather, as they considered the issue, the preterns had gained new insights into concepts of innovation and change on which they chose to focus their attention. The participants were learning that culture may be defined in terms of decisions about the allocation of time and resources and that what frequently passed for change within the school culture was merely a substitution of qualitatively similar activities within unaltered time slots.

The three preterns talked with many people who had worked with the children who were candidates for enrollment in Las Palmas. They discovered that these children were identified as "underachievers" within the context of their regular school program and that their lack of success in the area of reading was of particular concern. Change was clearly indicated. But if the available time was to be filled with something different and if that something was *to make a difference,* curricular decisions would have to be based upon reliable data. The preterns' own biases had to be kept in check.

Tina, Gail, and Boyd knew that the effectiveness of Las Palmas as an environment for learning was highly dependent upon the decisions they, themselves, were to make:

From readings, coursework, and past experiences we knew that environment would have to be one in which our preconceptions, assumptions, and values were not imposed on the children and their families. The perception by the children of our values (as reflected in the curriculum) as different from theirs would result in destructive ambiguity.

The variables to be controlled, then, were ourselves—our behavior, preconceptions, assumptions, and values. The environment that we would create would have to be one in which the children could communicate to us what they valued and wanted.

They summarized their conviction by stating that they could not define for any child or adult the purpose and the meaning of his life. They felt that they could only create conditions in which he could find his own purpose and meaning.

Boyd, Gail, and Tina saw their mission as one of *creating conditions,* and their minischool, Las Palmas, evolved as a project in which the creative search for conditions became the focus. Their task, as they saw it, was not one of creating a fixed product.

In April the three began visiting a Saturday morning program that they learned from its director was the only regular activity provided for local elementary-aged children:

The children seemed to be familiar with the set-up and most became involved in the art projects with a minimum of difficulty. Most of the children appeared to be Mexican-American, ranging in age from four to twelve years. We talked and played with the children, and were known to some by name by the third visit. As we evaluated Las Palmas as a possible minischool site, we felt that our association with the program director who was liked and respected by the children, would be a valuable asset in gaining their confidence. Her program would provide a flexible core based on positive community acceptance.

As the preterns took the steps necessary to secure official permission to use the community center for the minischool, they talked with various persons and had their initial impressions confirmed. Statistically, 70 percent of the project's residents were Mexican-American; there was one black family, and the rest were white. Another impression that was also confirmed in their contacts with the residents was that the housing project was a closed enclave that had little intercourse with city institutions and services. In the words of one informant, the housing project, embedded in a largely professional and middle-class community, was "The Great Forgotten." Gail, Tina, and Boyd felt an urgent need to ameliorate some of the effects of such an oversight. They made arrangements for use of the community center during the summer and then moved ahead with the prerequisites to "creating conditions":

After this initial stage of observation and selection of site, we began a series of interviews with Las Palmas residents and with persons involved in community work there. The purpose of these interviews was to find out what these people wanted in terms of a summer program. We would then base our goals for the summer on these findings, rather than imposing a particular set of beliefs based on our stereotype of the needs of a poverty community.

What the three discovered in their interviews confirmed for them the validity of the approach they had chosen. They found well-intentioned efforts of people in power who, though they struggled to transfer that power to the residents of the Las Palmas community, were far removed from the realities of its life. By failing to put themselves in position to hear the people's expression of their values and needs, they were contributing subtly to the problems they assiduously sought to alleviate.

The preterns perceived these relationships as a microcosmic example of the problems associated with all social change:

Las Palmas might even be seen as a ghetto in miniature, where the bitternesses and back-stabbings occur between individual people or ethnic groups rather than between huge poverty agencies and political organizations. When we began to see these cross-currents, which were definitely not apparent at first, we became much more cautious about what we said and did. We resolved not to be caught in this same syndrome of presumption about what needed to be done. The goals for the minischool would be determined by the needs expressed by the people of Las Palmas. The structure would impose no preconceived notions about what we would find there. Open-ended activities would allow the communication of values to come from the children without our intervention.

In their proposal for the minischool, Gail, Boyd, and Tina listed goals that emerged from the reported needs and concerns of the community. Their purpose was to create a structure that would facilitate the free communication of values by stimulating thought and language through oral and written communication. Their goals reflected the children's will to achieve in school. They envisioned open-ended art activities and story writing as a means by which children could express their own values while at the same time acquiring important skills and self-confidence in the purposeful use of these skills. Although the three encountered numerous roadblocks in their efforts to implement their program, they persevered.

A number of people warned that Las Palmas teenagers, for whom there were no planned activities, were likely to be disruptive. Although they sought only to work with elementary-aged children, Boyd, Gail, and Tina felt that the influence of the youth on their program and on the younger children for whom the teenagers were compelling models could not be ignored. Gang behavior with its potential for drug abuse posed a profound problem that could seriously thwart the minischool's purposes. Regarding this matter as one of prerequisite priority, the three preterns considered various alternatives. They developed contacts with Chicano college students and with the local Boys' Club and ultimately promoted the establishment of a teen program to keep the youth productively occupied during minischool hours.

Although Boyd spoke Spanish fluently, the trio recognized that cross-cultural communication involved more than bilingualism. They made an early commitment to community involvement by asking a woman who resided in Las Palmas to work with them as a paid staff member. They had been advised by several sources that the aide they selected would not only provide invaluable assistance on a day-to-day basis, but that this person would also serve as an important link to the target community.

The preterns believed in the importance of not imposing an alien climate upon the community if they were to discover the ethos that shaped it. By using the community house—with a rickety pingpong table set against one wall and with a picture of Christ mounted above a battered piano—the three accommodated to the environment in which the group life of the housing project's residents was lived: "It was a place where they had attended parties, taken their children to the clinic, sent their children to Sunday school, and held meetings." It was devoid of associations with the institutionalized school setting in which many of the project's children had met failure, and Boyd, Gail, and Tina determined to maintain this distance in curriculum as well as in physical arrangements and materials. Beside the necessary art supplies, a large portion of the preterns' allotted funds eventually went for theatrical makeup, materials for constructing costumes, and for ready-made "dress-up" clothes from thrift shops.

Planning for a creative environment was difficult, however. It was necessary for all materials and equipment to be stored in a workroom each noon, since the facility was used for other purposes during the afternoons and evenings. The three talked about the problem with an architectural student from a local university. He visited the site. This "environmental consultant," for a fee, designed and arranged for the construction of a large shelved cart that accommodated modular containers (shoe boxes) for supplies. The cart was the only new artifact the trio introduced into their minischool setting. They reasoned that the element of familiarity was an important one in developing and maintaining a comfortable environment.

The group avoided regarding their minischool as providing a solution to problems that result from sociological factors. They did not, for example, assume that a "male modeling curriculum" was needed simply because 68 percent of the project families were fatherless:

We were not in a position to say that a matriarchal society was either a problem or an asset. What we wanted was a structure and schedule in which the hopes, fears, traumas, and world views of the community members could surface and be communicated to us.

In June the three met for the first time with their "curriculum consultant," a person who had previously established two different alternative schools and who had taught in widely diverse cultural settings with notable success. In agreement with the general thrust of the minischool program, their consultant advised the group that all of their priorities might be incorporated into a program centered upon dramatic activities. Boyd, Gail, and Tina readily recognized that such a program would provide a means to achieve their goals of communication, language development, and community involvement.

Through drama the children would be encouraged to engage in enterprises that would allow their behavior to be observed legitimately. While the program's focus would provide direction, dramatic activity held potential for "open-endedness" since its conditions (costumes, makeup, and staging) could be determined by the children. The opportunity for improvisation within the basic structure of plot would enable the children to use language on behalf of their own needs. By encouraging each child's improvisations, the group felt they would be helping him to reify "his state of being, his values, and his culture" and to communicate these.

Although the children were known to have "reading problems," the three chose not to focus on language deficiencies. They felt that the weight of school experience had conveyed to the children the message that there was something wrong with their native language usage. Instead, language, defined as the multidimensional use of the written and spoken word, was viewed nonjudgmentally in the Las Palmas program. The trio decided that weekly dramatic presentations would offer the children a common experience upon which a child could differentiate. As they selected their own makeup and costumes, and improvised within the logic of the plot, the children would be able not only to express their own biographies, but also to transcend limitations of time, space, and reality. Boyd, Tina, and Gail saw in dramatic activities potential for cognitive growth through the process that Piaget identifies as "decentering." A child who plays in another's role must think from the viewpoint of the other person. Retrospectively, the three observed that in their minischool, this did indeed happen.

They also noted that their program provided conditions for the development of group solidarity and cooperation and for the just solution of problems that emerged. Interruption of play rehearsals led the children to establish a rule against door slamming and another that no one would be admitted to the building after a certain time in the morning. The desire to communicate to others something of the excitement that their endeavors produced resulted eventually in enthusiastic publication of a daily newspaper that Gail, Boyd, and Tina initiated the first minischool day. And parents—whether because their children told them about the plays or because they read about them in the newspaper—came to the play productions each Friday morning.

Despite the goals of its organizers, when the minischool program began, there was no commitment to participation on the part of any parent. Participation became a reality as parents came to join in the weekly celebrations. Gail, Tina, and Boyd felt that a sense of values shared with the adult community became stronger each week. Their goal of vertical participation was realized in its fullest expression on the final day of the minischool that was the occasion for a fiesta. Over 150 people—half of them parents—attended this event. All the food for the fiesta was prepared and served by mothers in the housing project. *None* of it was solicited by the minischool staff.

Boyd, Gail, and Tina attributed such a manifestation of involvement to the manner in which they approached achievement of all their goals. From the first day, they established a low profile as teachers in order that the children would react in terms of a self-regulatory group relationship rather than responding to the preterns as bearers of "Anglo" culture. They had decided to perpetuate the image of a program devoted to arts and crafts, as that was the image with which the children had become familiar:

As a few curious children came to the community center on Monday morning, they were greeted with rows of shoe boxes containing assorted materials for creative construction—scraps of paper, metal, wood, plastic, and foil. After ten minutes of wandering around the room and asking "What do we do?" "We're stupid. How do we do it?" the noise level dropped, and twenty-two children were sitting at two long tables, making constructions with their various materials.

On the opening day, the first of many trips to the library served a dual function. Primarily, the trips were intended to permit the children to choose books upon which they might base their plays. Secondly, the three preterns hoped to rally community support for their project by indicating that serious learning was expected to occur rather than merely "fun and games," which might have been regarded as frivolous:

The children went to the books as eagerly as they had seized upon the shoe boxes. . . . The books also provided the children with a structure. Rather than focusing on teacher direction, the children were to follow the logic of the plot. Again, this was in an effort to strengthen group cohesion and self-regulation. Within the existing structure of a book's story line, the children would feel safe enough to satisfy their inherent need to communicate to an audience.

For most of the children, the books chosen were familiar ones. Because the stories were old friends and self-selected, they were not threatening to the children and did serve, for the most part, to motivate playmaking:

When we arrived the next morning, five children were already waiting with books in hand. There was no need to remind them of the playmaking task. As other children trickled in, they found the original five children sitting together, reading their books to each other. Imitating this behavior, many settled down to the same task. In many cases, the younger children brought their books to us for reading. After about a half an hour, groups began to emerge. The younger children were listening to Gail read a story, the boys were centered around Boyd, and the seven- to nine-year-old girls were reading with Tina.

These three groups remained fairly constant during the entire first week. They evolved primarily due to the initial selection of different play material by the group members. However, with so many books chosen, the first dramatic efforts needed constant refocusing by the three preterns. An account of Gail's experience with the younger children shows some of the difficulties that were experienced during the first stimulating week:

The four- to six-year-olds' selection of books had been random and excited in the library, and their behavior continued in this general vein. Because the children could not focus on any book, Gail chose a story with a simple plot filled with action. This new focus was only partially successful as Gail had to constantly remind the children of the task at hand. Restless behavior and comments such as, "I don't want to be a monkey. I want to be a lady," indicated to us that the children were not wedded to the playmaking. The story had been introduced out of necessity by a force outside their group.

Additionally, the open-endedness the preterns had so deliberately planned meant that attendance was neither regular nor sustained. Children, including younger brothers and sisters, came and went. By mid-week, five or so new children arrived to participate in the activities, and the play the younger children were preparing for the Friday performance had, except for one child, a whole new cast. As new children arrived, Gail attempted to involve them immediately in the production by introducing the idea that a play required making costumes and props. The costumes helped focus the children on their roles, and the rehearsals proceeded with greater seriousness.

Tina confronted a different kind of problem. Her group of girls chose a story they had all read in school the previous year. Despite their familiarity with it, however, they had difficulty with their reading. Eventually, however, they called on Tina for help. She assisted the girls in reading and rereading their selection until they felt satisfied that they had it under their control. When this point was reached, the group decided they were ready to make it into a play: Parts were easily decided upon, as the girls were very cooperative. Practice was serious and concentrated and continued that way through Wednesday. When one of the girls brought a younger sister, a new part was created for her, and the girls rehearsed the play three times before asking to make costumes or to practice with makeup. They considered their roles carefully as they searched for their various costumes.

The boys Boyd was working with presented a different set of interests. Some were expressed quite strongly and with independence:

Danny and his younger brother Frank were concerned with dinosaurs. Neither of these two boys were interested in playmaking. Jaime, who was interested, left the group and joined Gail's group, which was already underway. Because Boyd was interested in seeing how the group's interests would emerge, he allowed the restlessness and ambivalence to work itself out. After a while, his boys seized on the costumes and began parading around the rooms with calls of "I am the king."

Little persuasion was needed, though, before the boys were incorporated into focal activities. Boyd offered them surplus materials to be reshaped into chairs and painted for the dramatic productions. However, when this task was completed, the boys joined several newcomers in wandering around, tussling, and slamming doors.

Accepting the children's fragmented definition of the social situation, the preterns each took responsibility for supervising a cluster of children and for trying to respond to demonstrated interests. At the same time as they accommodated to the children, they worked to build a time and activity structure that would provide the children with dependable expectations. The establishment of a daily rhythm would, they felt, not only lay a foundation for the weeks to follow, it would also provide a matrix in which to observe children so that the program might be shaped to their needs.

Despite evidence that the children were capable of self-involvement, the three preterns nonetheless noted a general tendency toward guardedness and hesitancy. The first week was fraught with unanticipated difficulties that required of the preterns a level of restraint and patience that ran counter to their aspirations and their enthusiasm. A group of older girls who had participated in the former recreation program took a proprietory and elitist attitude toward the program; their jockeying for special privilege militated against the cohesiveness the preterns sought to foster. While the older boys easily incorporated newcomers and demonstrated procedures to them, much of their time throughout the week, along with that of newly arrived children, was spent in testing Boyd's orientation and his relationship to them.

Initiation into the newspaper activity met with a suggestion of resistance when eight-year-old Donna said, "I don't like newspapers. ... They talk about poor people in newspapers." The preterns recognized that the children's experience with the news had shown them only that it was hostile to their world and demeaning to their people. Boyd, Gail, and Tina inferred that the idea of printed media being employed as a means of self-expression was an unfamiliar one to these children. The brevity and impersonality of the youngsters' account of the first morning's experience attested to their insecurity:

TODAY 20 PEOPLE CAME TO ART SCHOOL. THERE WERE 12 BOYS AND 10 GIRLS. WE MADE STUFF OUT OF BOXES.

WE ARE GOING TO THE LIBRARY TODAY AND GET BOOKS. THE BOOKS WILL GIVE US IDEAS FOR PLAYS.

As it turned out not all of the children were interested in direct involvement in dramatic activities. They seemed to accept indirect ways of participating, however. Danny's skill at classification, which had shown itself in relation to prehistoric reptiles, was put in the service of organizational tasks: "He did not enjoy the drama, but did work successfully at classifying and sorting materials and props."

Like some of the boys, the older girls at first refused to adapt to the developing rhythm; they responded favorably to the idea of being responsible for refreshments, however. They spent Wednesday baking cookies in the kitchen, and in the weeks that followed they seized upon this role whenever they were not creating plays of their own.

While the newspaper period on Wednesday followed the general pattern of the two previous days, references to children by name, the recounting of events, and the stating of future plans showed that the children were becoming more comfortable with the program and with each other, as well as with the printed word as a means of communication. By Thursday, Tina, Gail, and Boyd felt that a rhythm had begun to establish itself:

Thursday was dress rehearsal day. That fact infused the group with a common purpose. The newspaper for the day is clear indication of the group cohesion. While the two play groups were rehearsing and perfecting their costumes and makeup, the boys decided that the actors needed quiet and took a walk with Boyd to collect art materials. When they returned, they made invitations for the following day. During the newspaper period, the children who were not involved in plays took roles for the next day. The older girls would serve refreshments; the boys would help set up. It is interesting that the art work and many of the comments in the newspaper were made by children who had been uninvolved and disruptive the day before.

Friday's newspaper proclaimed it to be "the big day" and heralded an event that produced a general feeling of excitement, anticipation, and apprehension. When Boyd, Gail, and Tina arrived at nine o'clock, twenty-five children were waiting for them. After the younger children had finished their last practice, they ran to get their mothers. "It was," the preterns noted, "as if they had not quite believed that the plays would ever take place." The presence of a photographer and a reporter from the local paper indicated that they, indeed, had produced something of value:

The children were proud and excited. They understood that the plays were of their own doing, that everyone had contributed to the group effort. The energy and cohesion that had been released was evident when we met again on Tuesday, July 6. When given watercolors, most of the children proceeded to paint pictures of the plays. The boys, who had not acted the week before, began, without prompting, to write their own play. When we made our trip to the library Tuesday, the children were much more selective and concentrated, and asked us for advice as to what stories might make good plays.

Additionally, on the second Tuesday, the preterns experienced what they regarded as a major breakthrough with the community. Although, during their planning of the minischool, they had offered to employ one of the mothers as an aide, she had waited the entire first week before visiting the school:

She had evidently been observing us throughout the week. After the Friday plays, she had been sufficiently convinced of the program's validity for the children of her community. On Tuesday she volunteered her help. She was an invaluable member of the staff throughout the program.

While their aide was enthusiastic and supportive, Boyd, Gail, and Tina had no way of knowing whether she represented community feeling. An increasing number of parents attending the Friday performances was the only indication of community acceptance. However, as the weeks progressed, the preterns were gratified to observe the children's increasing communication of themselves:

More and more volunteered to write for the newspaper. Original stories, pictures dealing with culturally important symbols such as homes, priests, and churches, problems experienced in the minischool, and children's feelings and opinions were published. Most importantly, stories written in Spanish were interspersed throughout. On library trips, the children showed independent and highly motivated behavior. They seemed to know what they wanted. Many asked specifically for Spanish books. Others went directly to certain sections, chose their books, and read quietly for half an hour or asked that their books be read to them. During art projects, the children were relaxed and concentrated. With little direction from us, they made a varied and imaginative assortment of puppets during the third and fourth weeks.

Dramatic presentations also revealed the children's growing ability to express themselves. Many of the children needed some guidance from us throughout the entire project. Therefore, they chose to participate in large productions in which we acted as facilitators. However, these children were able to keep to the task, to follow the logic of the plot, and to improvise within it without significant redirection from us. In their production of "The Musicians of Bremen," for example, the children chose to translate the dialogue into Spanish. As the weeks progressed, more and more children broke away from the group and created their own plays.

Gail, Boyd, and Tina considered the introduction of Spanish to be an especially significant manifestation of the children's cultural identities and their desire to open themselves to their minischool teachers. Growth in group cohesiveness was evident throughout the six weeks. In a written critique of their project, the participants cited specific examples of behavior that indicated to them that such growth had occurred during the course of the minischool program:

Luci was a very shy eight-year-old. The other girls excluded her from their activities, and on the first day they taunted her because she had been retained in school. Luci was an outcast. The production of the first play, however, was proof to Luci and to the other children that she was important. Luci became a confident leader and took part in subsequent productions. In the second week she began speaking fluent Spanish as well as English. Other children followed her example.

Each child was quite concerned during the first week that the other children were getting more art supplies or a larger portion of snacks than he was. This situation created much tension and confusion. The children soon realized that there were enough supplies and snacks for everyone. Snacktime became a relaxed break when the children sat and talked about the day's activities. Art became a time for children to concentrate on their own projects rather than to hoard materials.

Two six-year-old boys were ignored by everyone during the first three days of the project. They stood outside the room and watched the activities of the other children. On Thursday of the first week, it was pointed out by an older child that the two boys had nothing to do. The older children soon involved them in the day's activities. Both participated in play productions the following week.

Attesting to the validity of the program provided for the children as well as the growing magnanimity of the group was the minischool's constantly increasing enrollment. By its final week over fifty children were in regular attendance. Toward the end of July, a trip to Los Angeles for a presentation by the Ballet Folklorico de Mexico provided the catalyst that stimulated the children to plan the fiesta on the final day and to make that day their own:

The children were entranced by this expression of their culture. Their subli-mated cultural identity resonated to the splendid costumes and vigorous move-ment of the dancers. The aspects of celebration and dance had now been ex-perienced by and legitimized for the children. They demanded to recreate the immediacy of the experience at Las Palmas.

Mona and Lolita, recent immigrants from Mexico, could not speak English. Eager to communicate with the other children, they presented an exquisite expression of their identity at the community center on Thursday. They brought records and skirts from home and taught their friends a Mexican dance. This was exactly the expression of values we had hoped would surface. We stepped back and observed its function.

Thursday's newspaper indicated the depth of the children's response. Fif-teen children, many of whom were contributing for the first time, published stories and self-portraits. A fiesta was mentioned.

On Friday the children planned the fiesta. They suggested games, a dance and drama presentation, an art display, all culminating in a community feast. Whereas their desire to share art and drama grew out of the minischool experi-ence, their focus on games, dance, and food was an intense expression of their own biographies. We viewed this as their need to relive directly or symbolically their reservoir of shared values and sentiments.

The children chose to re-enact the play which both actors and audience had most enjoyed. They held several rehearsals throughout the week. The children's choice of games reflected their experience in the carnivals and church bazaars of their own culture. A group of boys spent the next week building booths and painting equipment necessary for the games. Mona and Lolita took charge of the dancing. It was soon evident that a vital element to the dancing was missing: the costumes. Each girl was given the opportunity to select materials and trim-mings for a skirt which she then completed during the week.

On Friday, Gail, Tina and Boyd were overwhelmed by the community's response to the children's preparations. They recalled that they had been unsure of their ability as outsiders to stimulate the community toward recreating its own sense of shared values and therefore had settled on a narrow definition of community participation: primarily parent audiences at the weekly plays. But the abundance of food that mothers brought throughout the morning and the long tables provisioned to feed 150 people represented a medium of communi-cation that they had not dreamed of nor conceptualized in their minischool proposal:

Communication had been our goal: the children communicated on one level needs and values through their efforts in drama; on another level were the public communications—the newspaper and the weekly dramatic offerings. But the Fiesta demonstrated a new element and level of communication—that of people celebrating together a common sense of community, the depth and subtlety of which we may yet be unaware.

Boyd, Tina, and Gail had believed that as "white Anglos" they could create an environment in which minority children would be able to learn. When they created the Las Palmas minischool they tested that belief. Their program attested to the validity of their approach—that is, to learn from children. They did that. They learned so much more at Las Palmas than they had expected they would. Mostly they learned a lot about themselves.

10 Ramona

Maxine and Helga took seriously the questions with which they were confronted in the spring when they decided to plan and conduct their minischool together. Everything that they had been considering individually had to be "rethought and decided upon." The issue at hand was whether, in six weeks, they could create a learning environment in which children could feel comfortable enough to reach out to new experience and to become confident users of tools for self expression.

Practically oriented, they focused first upon functional problems related to the operation of the project: "In what community should we work? What kinds of feelings would the community have about schooling in general? Where can we find a centrally located building or other inexpensive housing? What kinds of community services should be included in the program? How shall we allocate our $692.00? Should it be for supplies, field trips, hardware, aides, consultants, rent, or transportation? Should we use volunteers and if so in what ways?" Eventually these questions led them to the most crucial question of all: "What goals do we wish to accomplish and for whom?"

In attempting to find answers to this primary question, others followed about program and the curriculum to be planned. Helga and Maxine had certain criteria and specifications in mind. They wanted to work in a low-income area, preferably a point of entry for Mexican immigrants. They also wished to be at a location where the people were receiving services through social agencies, and hence some of the basic needs of the population had already been defined and were being met. The preterns could then devote themselves to strictly educational matters.

Maxine, during the spring, had worked in a nearby town of about 17,500 people, of which about 25 percent were Mexican-American. There were other groups of Dutch, German, and Basque ancestry. The town was originally established as a farming community; now it was a large dairy center.

Maxine had become acquainted with a housing project, Ramona, in the town while doing her practicum at a public school. Along with other projects with which they were not as familiar, Helga and Maxine considered Ramona as a possibility and finally chose it as their site. Ramona was built in the fifties by the U.S. Government for people of low incomes. Composed of forty-nine units, it now housed forty-seven families. The two unoccupied units had been converted to other uses. One was now a community apartment and the other a health clinic. The rents at Ramona varied and were based upon family size,

109

income, and number of bedrooms in the apartment. The housing project office was a medium-sized room adjacent to a patio and outdoor space that could be used for a variety of activities. This arrangement looked inviting to the preterns and appeared to be an excellent setting for the minischool. When this complex was offered rent free to the preterns by the project manager, they were elated.

Having identified their community and site, the two began to talk with various people associated with the service programs already established. The director of the federal housing project helped them broaden their acquaintance with community residents. The director of the Council of Social Services (for the project), with whom Maxine had worked before, supplied them with background information about the community and with the names of people who would serve as contacts for field trips and as resources for the program. The coordinator of the Occupational Education Center assigned a Neighborhood Youth Corps teenager to work in the minischool; happily she was bilingual and a project resident. Additionally, the housing director gave the two young women the names and addresses of all the resident families and the ages of their children. Although he offered them the use of the community office rent free, he explained that they would have to vacate the center when other, already scheduled, service groups had need of the facility.

Maxine and Helga knew that their personally recruiting the children and families who would be involved in their program would be necessary. Before they went went from house to house to meet with potential participants, however, they decided to contact the local primary and elementary school offices and talk over with the principals their plans for an alternative school. Since they hoped to offer another style of education, they did not wish to alienate public school officials by not letting them know their intentions in advance. Maxine and Helga did not anticipate what was to follow. Instead of welcoming the two novices, the principals and other district administrators clearly considered their operation to be "competition" and a threat to the established district programs, and inquiries were made about legal means of stopping the minischool being planned by Helga and Maxine. An obvious problem was that if the minischool were allowed to flourish, it might draw students from the traditional summer session in the district, which would lose the vital state funds supplied to it on the basis of average daily attendance.

To counteract the opposition based on this problem, the women appealed to the Board of Education to make their minischool an "official" function of the local schools. In that way the district would receive its state money for the children who attended the alternative school, and Helga and Maxine would be free to operate without opposition. The local district administrators agreed to consider the two preterns as "volunteer student teachers" and to "supervise" them during the summer of operation. Furthermore, the local schools would supply the two young women with many of the teaching materials they would need. The preterns, for their part, would keep careful records of attendance so that the district might be reimbursed. On balance, the arrangement would benefit everyone although Maxine and Helga had not wished to emphasize "attendance" in their minischool.

Maxine and Helga decided to limit enrollment in the minischool to residents of the project for two reasons. First, they believed a social boundary, reinforced by an insular arrangement of the buildings and apartments, seemed to exist between the people who lived in Ramona and those outside of it. Second, the two wished to develop a sense of community and "family" among the children and to substitute a positive feeling of identity for the negative one the children appeared to hold. Maxine and Helga hoped through their planned activities and supportive emotional climate to develop a sense of camaraderie and productive, cooperative endeavor.

Theoretically, the preterns planning a minischool could decided upon any grouping or age-mixture of children. A school could include young people from one to twenty or it could be restricted to a very narrow age range, even one year. After briefly considering establishing twelfth grade as the school's upper limit, Helga and Maxine decided to accept only children of elementary school who had finished at least first grade. In this way, they hoped to avoid the problem of teaching the beginning reader.

The preterns distributed the following notice and went from apartment to apartment to meet each family.

MINISCHOOL
An Alternative Summer School Program

Offering activities and individualized instruction in reading, math, science, social studies, media, and art.

> *WHO: All children who have completed first through sixth grade.*
> *WHEN: June 28th through August 6, Monday-Friday, 8:30-11:30 a.m.*
> *WHERE: The Community Hall and surroundings.*

MINI-ESCUELA
Un programa alternativo de la Escuela del Verano

Se ofrecen actividades e instrucción individualizada en la lectura, la matemática, las ciencias, los estudios sociales, la comunicación, y el arte.

> *¿Quién?: Todos los niños los cuales han cumplido el primer grado hasta el sexto grado quedan invitados a participar.*
> *¿Cuándo?: El 28 de junio al 6 de agosto, los lunes a viernes, desde las 8:30 horas hasta las 11:30 horas.*
> *¿Dónde?: El Centro Comunal y la vecindad.*

Since Maxine was fluent in Spanish, the team could converse in whichever language a family felt comfortable. They explained their program in familiar, conservative terms since they did not wish to frighten the recent immigrants from Mexico, who they felt had trust in the traditional American educational system.

The preterns were somewhat disappointed in the results of their interviews. Some families, they found, were planning summer vacations and would be away for substantial periods of time. Others had already enrolled their children in the regular district summer session and could not be persuaded to change their minds. Many of the children, when asked, made clear that they did not want to attend *any* school during the summer recess. After visiting almost all the residents, the two young women obtained twenty-eight "registrations" out of fifty-six possibilities.

Maxine and Helga were anxious to enlist as many adult helpers as possible. An aide from a nearby school heard about the summer experiment and volunteered to help. One of Claremont's regular teaching interns became intrigued with the venture and asked whether he could fulfill his summer practicum by working at Ramona. Several parents also volunteered from time to time, especially when field trips were being planned.

Through clever staffing and luck, the preterns found that they did not have to use their money for salaries but could reserve it instead for field trips, professional consultants, and supplies. Their final budget included:

Secretarial help:	$ 5.00
Transportation:	$ 50.00
Lecturers and consultants:	$ 50.00
Communication:	$ 10.00
Rentals:	$ 50.00
Supplies:	$527.00
Total	$692.00

The preterns started out with some general learning goals they intended to modify after they had had time to become acquainted with the children. Their general objectives reflected the young women's knowledge of child development, the culture of poverty, and the work they had done the previous year.

Helga and Maxine's greatest desire was to help each child develop a more positive self-image through sharpened communication skills. By encouraging them to help others and in turn to accept help from their peers, the preterns felt that the children might see the importance of participation within a group and obtain satisfaction from working interdependently.

By encouraging a free exchange of information and feelings, the two preterns hoped to increase the children's ability to use language. The team also wanted to provide the minischool students with such a satisfying experience that, by the end of the summer, they would have positive feelings about their ability to learn. With this optimistic orientation the children would have more confidence to undertake independent learning activities in their day-to-day lives, including the time spent in "regular" schools.

Being receptive to new and different experiences would help widen each child's "perspective of life," the preterns reasoned. Through experimentation with the arts in a safe environment, Maxine and Helga felt this objective might be reached. Free use of paints, crayons, cut paper, wood, musical instruments, and film might be the way to aesthetic satisfaction and to confidence. The two wanted to promote further reaching out and experimentation. Risk-taking behavior was to be encouraged, nourished, and reinforced.

Children who can work independently and follow through on tasks once undertaken gain self confidence, the two preterns felt. They were determined to provide experiences that would help their small group of children have the satisfaction of completing the jobs they began. By thorough familiarity with each child, the preterns expected to provide all with appropriate activities and to encourage completion of work, thus preventing frustration and feelings of failure.

Frequent walking trips into the neighborhood were planned in order to make the youngsters comfortable with the many resources available to them in the community. A film project was planned that would also encourage the children to venture beyond the housing project to make a visual record of what they had seen. At the minischool they would assimilate the experience by editing the film into a permanent record.

Besides a medium-sized room, a fenced-in patio that was partially cemented and covered, and a spacious lawn, the minischool facilities included a kitchen with a refrigerator, stove, and lockable storage cabinets. The preterns wished the children to move freely from one area to another and decided to divide the available space according to the nature of the activities; they planned to provide reflective and quiet zones, work areas, and social areas where the children could play games, talk freely, and generally socialize with their friends. In the library area they placed a couch, two rockers, a rug, and lots of books. Nearby were tables containing two typewriters, dictionaries, and other writing equipment. Since the children would have no assigned desks, and indeed there would not be enough desks for each child to have one, a shoe box was provided in which each child would keep his personal things.

The outside patio was designated as a creative workshop for arts, crafts, and carpentry. Maxine and Helga planned to take full advantage of the kitchen for cooking activities, and to use the lawn for organized sports, folk dancing, and the filming of movies with the 8mm camera they had purchased. A costume trunk and the cameras were to be placed on the patio as a central focus for the summer activities. Using these materials the children would explore different life roles and discover new media through which they could express their thoughts, feelings, and ideas.

The curriculum, as it evolved, was concentrated in several areas. The first dealt with the use of art media. Tie-dyeing, paper crafts, piñata making, and potato printing, all were designed to help the children develop control over their physical environment. The preterns believed these activities would enrich the children's sensory awareness, increase their means for individual expression, and ultimately help to enrich their spoken and written vocabularies.

Study of the neighborhood was another central theme. At least once a week Helga and Maxine planned walking trips within and around the project. The courthouse, fire station, library, garden nursery, and so forth were all potential places of interest that the children might come to view with a new perspective. The two preterns felt that by increasing the children's knowledge of the community, its history, its business, and its people, they would be better prepared to function productively within their environment.

Cooking, carpentry, and sewing were activities designed to provide the children with satisfying experiences and to promote the acquisition of fundamental skills. Art and music would be links to their cultural heritage. Records and phonographs would be continuously available.

The preterns scheduled time for storywriting, reading, puppetry, and plays. They hoped the children would find a comfortable mode for organizing their thoughts and feelings and be able to communicate them to others. There were many "tools of self-expression" the children could use. If they wished to talk about their ideas, tape recorders were available. If writing their thoughts was more comfortable, they could do so by themselves or they could enlist the help of one of the adults. The children could draw pictures or use still or movie cameras if they wished.

In their planning, Helga, Maxine, and Bob (their "student teacher") allocated their time in large blocks. In this way they hoped to provide the children with enough individual freedom to pursue their unique interests.

A daily snack time was regarded as nutritionally essential. Additionally, it would provide a reason for getting together as a community to share feelings and experiences. Thursday snacks were to be special, since the children were to plan a common menu and prepare the food. An extended sharing period on Fridays was to be a time for reliving the events of the week and planning for the next one.

School began late in June. Planning continued, however, in a comfortable, informal way. Each day, Maxine, Helga, and their student teacher, Bob, sat down with sack lunches and discussed the events of the morning. Often children would leave for home at noon and return shortly thereafter with younger siblings to share the luncheon session and provide their own opinions and suggestions for modifying the program.

The first week provided a number of surprises to the minischool group.

Instead of the calm free flow of activities, which had been planned, there was a booming, buzzing confusion. The lunchtime planning session during the first week was spent in modifying the preplanned program and making it a creative, viable enterprise by considering each child. The original program that had been sketched only in broad generalities had not been detailed minutely. Now each child was considered as an individual and his or her temperament, interests, and abilities were taken into account. The interns observed:

I guess especially because we had the span from first to sixth grades, there was no way you could put all the kids in one bag. The differences in children really stood out. . . . You've got to get to know them and they've got to get to know you before you can become really, truly sensitive to their needs and pick up on things.

In spite of the differences in the abilities and interests of the children, the preterns noticed a common characteristic among them. When they were left on their own, the boys and girls seemed to show "a lack of commitment" to completing a task. To help the youngsters experience a sense of achievement, the preterns recognized a need for increased close guidance, and they organized more tightly structured individual and group activities.

For Helga and Maxine who were committed to the concept of open learning environments, "tightening it up" entailed a certain psychological risk: Were they compromising their convictions? Were they "selling out" in order to buy safety for themselves? They discovered that they were not, since the children had as great a need for definition and limits as they did. In response to the observed behavior of the children, the preterns eventually restructured their program by making both time and place more ordered than originally planned; the result was an environment where children and adults were all able to engage in teaching and learning encounters that were stimulating *and* comfortable.

In family-like settings, Maxine, Helga, and Bob each took responsibility for a small group of children. The activities for each group differed according to its identified needs. Helga's group worked to discover numerical concepts by measuring for carpentry and by working with things like blocks, thermometers, and Cuisinaire rods. They recorded their observations on charts. Bob, whose group was composed mostly of younger children, centered his activities around reading and listening to stories. Maxine's group of predominantly older children seemed interested in writing but often found it difficult to begin. Maxine and her teenaged aide discovered that they could give the children the encouragement they needed by sitting down and beginning to write themselves. Given courage in an atmosphere of trust, the children became sufficiently confident that some of them dictated stories in Spanish and found to their amazement that, although they had never read Spanish before, they could read the stories back after they had been transcribed.

When the children had finished with the planned activities in their "family" groups, they were asked to commit themselves to other activities for the morning. Each day a new chart showed the choices available. These might include carpentry, sewing, film making, puppetry, story writing, reading, neighborhood walks, or specially arranged activities. By requiring the children to select from among specified choices, the preterns were helping them to begin to plan for the future and to structure the course of their own lives. In letting the children carry out their own plans, the preterns felt that they were closest to fulfilling their own mission.

Through exposure to new experiences in a familiar setting, the children began "coming out of themselves." The groups provided the security of a family situation that Helga and Maxine felt was necessary if the children eventually were going to explore the unfamiliar: "To explore you have to feel comfortable in your own little circle where you live. Then you can go beyond and search for more."

One of the novel experiences in which the children participated was film making. The idea of using a movie camera at Ramona had occurred to the preterns early in their planning, and they had bought an 8mm camera with some of the money they had budgeted for equipment. They introduced the camera to the children with some trepidation for they realized that they were taking a real risk that this expensive equipment could be broken at any time.

The first few days they demonstrated a number of times how the camera worked. When they felt reasonably assured that the children knew how to operate it, they left it in the bookcase to be used. Miraculously it remained intact throughout the summer. Each night Maxine and Helga took the film to be processed so that it would be available quickly.

At first a few of the children used the camera hesitantly. Early experimentation consisted of photographing anything at random, whether animate or inanimate. When the film was developed the children had no difficulty identifying such familiar objects as tables and trees captured on film, but they had a hard time recognizing themselves. The next stage of film production concentrated on short episodes that involved motion, such as handstands and somersaults. Then about the second weekend of the program, an event occurred that fostered a major breakthrough in the children's use of film. A wedding, attended by most of the children, was held at the Ramona Community Center. The youngsters were impressed with the color and pagentry of the event, and someone on Monday morning suggested that the group hold and photograph their own wedding ceremony. Since realism seemed important to the children, Maxine and Helga decided to let each of them have fifty cents from the supply budget for dress-up clothes from the neighborhood thrift store. They all went shopping in order to purchase properties for the production.

The success of the endeavor convinced the preterns that film was not only a vehicle for creative expression, but also a viable medium for helping the children "concretize in their minds" their ideas and feeling about their daily experiences. It whetted the children's appetite for more sophisticated cinematic adventures than they had yet undertaken. Ultimately they decided to write their own script and tell their own story. The scenario dealt with the perpetration of a bank robbery, and the final production, which was shown at the open house the last week of school, was reminiscent of the many television dramas that filled the children's lives. What made it different, however, was that the robbers triumphed in the end and sped off into the dusty sunset with the loot.

A special performance of the Mexican Ballet Folklorico that the children attended struck another responsive chord. Folk dancing quickly became a major activity at Ramona as the children tried to duplicate the dances they had seen. The preterns, to reinforce this interest, invited the town's children's librarian to come and help the group learn some of the dances. Dancing became a part of life in the minischool for the rest of its duration.

Cooking was also a popular activity. A favorite recipe, which made one pancake, was tried by each child. The products of other cooking projects were often enjoyed at snack time when the menu might include pudding, cupcakes, or candied apples.

Most of the children tried out many of the opportunities and activities available to them, but there were some who seemed to persist with one. Tony spent the summer making wooden crosses. Herrold loved to draw blue spiders. Some of the older boys spent most of their time playing records. Although the preterns hoped each child would take advantage of the varied activities available, the developmental clocks of some children were not paced for this to happen in six weeks.

The last week of school, Maxine, Helga, Bob, and the children decided to plan an open house to which they would invite all the project residents. The children decorated their center with the products of the summer and sent out invitations. Their mothers supplemented the refreshments they prepared for the event. The night of the open house they premiered their movie, which was a huge success. Rosa and her father brought their accordians, and spontaneously, the whole gathering had an informal dance session that ended with everyone doing the bunny hop. The preterns had difficulty convincing the parents that the children had learned anything during the program since they had had so much fun.

At the end of the evening of the open house, when the preterns and some volunteers were cleaning up, they discovered that one of the tape players was missing. In the morning they tacked notices on tree trunks in the housing project. Within an hour the tape player was back in the bookcase from which it had been taken.

On reflection, Maxine and Helga were both proud of what they had done and frustrated that they had not been able to do more. There just had not been enough time to accomplish all they had set out to do. They realized that they had attempted to include in a six-week program a staggering array of activities: visits to the community, field trips, carpentry, and other creative activities in addition to skill-building sessions. While they acknowledged the overambitiousness of their program, their lack of experience, and the limitations of time, they felt a sense of elation at what they had accomplished:

Today is the last day of school. I don't feel the same as you usually feel. I'm kind of glad it's over because it's finished–something you've done, planned, accomplished. But I'd be willing to start again on Monday!

11 The Urban Studies Workshop

While the planners of one minischool each retained a strong identification with his own ethnic and cultural roots, they shared a common experience with the shortcomings of schools within urban settings:

Even though our backgrounds are different in many respects, we had little trouble in finding common ground in our realization of the need for positive input into the crisis faced by the American educational system.

Clive, an Afro-American, Ben, a Jewish-American, and Stu, a Russian-American, stood upon that common ground when, at the end of the summer, they described and evaluated their own "positive input": the Urban Studies Workshop. This minischool project was designed for youth who were experiencing a sense of alienation within the traditional school setting. It had been developed on the premise that a different kind of program could make a difference in their perception of themselves and the usefulness of learning. The planners believed that adolescents also have a need for economic independence. They wanted to help a multiracial group of young people discover that they each could make a valued contribution to group life in the wider community.

Problems experienced by black adolescents in a white-dominated society had engrossed the trio throughout the preceding year. They saw black students as victims of prejudicial treatment caused by the middle-class values and expectations held by their teachers. The participants asserted, "It is safe to say that many black school children are unable to learn because they are not taught." To be "taught," they felt, a student must be confronted with real-life problems with which he can identify.

During the year at Claremont, each of the three participants had involved himself extensively in the classroom programs of nearby high schools that were undergoing a period of racial conflict and violence. They had been shocked by the intensity of feeling that inflamed both teachers and students. The black studies courses they were taking concurrently with their field work cast these experiences into a social-psychological, as well as historical, perspective, which they elaborated upon in establishing a rationale for their minischool program.

Although the participants were preoccupied with the crisis in black community schools, they saw this crisis as indicative of problems throughout the country's education system and established a multi-ethnic, multiracial minischool. Following the termination of their minischool program, they wrote of

119

factors contributing to the alienation of blacks and then added:

We are also aware that there are problems of inexperienced teachers, class conflict, and lack of community control in Chicano and white communities. It remains our goal to do all we are capable of doing to help rectify these problems. Thus did we establish our summer "minischool," the Urban Studies Workshop, with the thought in mind that however small in origin, it could be of significant value in creating greater understanding among the diverse ethnic groups—to let them know of their common problems and common bond.

Their experience in public schools had convinced the three participants that the problems of racial conflict could be solved only if they brought students together who were affected by them. They saw alienation as resulting in further disaffection between groups, a consequence that contributed to the problems instead of to solutions. Therefore, a major goal of the workshop's program was to create greater understanding among the diverse groups living in the community where the minischool was located and awareness of the need for interdependence.

From the time that Ben, Stu, and Clive began working in the community's secondary schools, there was never any doubt that their minischool would be located close by. They wanted the students they had come to know to be able to experience the value of diversity and of working together instead of at cross-purposes. They explained this decision as follows:

It was our opinion that the world is made up of many different kinds of people and that every effort should be made to develop meaningful lines of communication between them. Therefore, along with our desire for a "racially balanced" school, we also sought diversity in other ways: students who were academically inclined, as well as those who had little interest in books or school; students who could read at acceptable levels and those who could not; students who were artistically inclined and those who were not. In developing the Urban Studies Workshop we sought to create a small-scale society involving as many different kinds of people as we could find.

They found the diversity they sought among youthful friends in the school situations in which they participated during the year. Ten blacks, five whites, and seven brown youths made up the student body of the Urban Studies Workshop. Together, and with the help of the preterns, these students mounted an attack upon problems common to all their lives. Together, they spent a lively summer doing things that made sense to each of them as individuals.

Ben, Clive, and Stu knew they wanted to capitalize upon diversity in their minischool. They knew, too, that they would locate the school *within* the community. These were easy decisions to reach, and as commitments, they were made early, before detailed plans were worked out. Other decisions required considerably more time and thought. The three participants underwent many experiences throughout the year upon which they reflected critically in order to establish criteria for their own program.

Although located in geographical proximity to the neighborhoods in which students live, schools often are psychologically and socially remote from the people and their concerns, Stu, Ben, and Clive observed. They regarded this distance as one that is reinforced both by curricular irrelevance to surrounding environments and lifestyles and by physical restraints to a free exchange among people and ideas. They noted that the closed-campus policy of many high schools establishes a prison-like atmosphere that "separates and isolates the school activities from those of the community, and in many ways, prevents one from influencing the other."

As the participants visited school programs and contributed large amounts of their own time to working within them—especially during a spring practicum period when their own plans were in formative stages—they noticed a common phenomenon: "The student may learn quite a bit about the city government of Washington D.C., but know little of the structure or dynamics of his own [city or community]—which to a far greater degree affects his life." The three commented that a result of this academic approach is that a student has little knowledge to cope with what he faces when he leaves school at two o'clock each afternoon. The participants felt that in his schooling, the student *"has been made unprepared"* [emphasis added] not only for personal fulfillment, but also for economic survival:

We wanted our project to provide an alternative to this existing situation. Rather than having a fence we wanted an open door. Rather than being isolated from the community we wanted to have as much community involvement and input as possible. We felt by doing this we could bring our academic program in touch with the community and our students' lifestyles.

Clive, Ben, and Stu regarded as essential developing an intimate familiarity with their students and with their ways of living. During their year in public schools, the three men were saddened to find that within the school setting students were not the only people experiencing a fragmented existence. Teachers were not regarded as "whole" persons either; the participants felt they played various roles, which usually involved taking an authoritarian stance:

Students have little chance to know the person behind the role. Rarely do they see him eat or go to the restroom. . . . What results is very little two-way communication. Fear and distrust are often outcomes. . . . The student fears risk taking in exploring new ideas and new knowledge. Meaningful learning cannot take place under these conditions.

For trust to develop, according to the participants:

A teacher must come to know his pupils and his pupils must come to know him. . . . They must be able to see him in many different moods, in a variety of contexts, and, at times, in a most personal way. He must come across as a human being. This is something they understand as compared to some distant figure performing in a threatening role.

Ben, Stu, and Clive hoped to break down the traditionally perceived role of the teacher by exposing themselves as people who were not infallible, but who had strengths *and* weaknesses, just as their students did. They recognized that openness and honesty involved emotional risk to themselves. But they regarded their own self-exposure and vulnerability as essential to a relationship with students in which two-way communication could flourish.

The three men used every presented opportunity to get to know the young people better. When such an opportunity did not occur naturally, they contrived to create one, and they built upon casual contact with students to develop relationships that were sustained in out-of-school circumstances. They looked upon the high school students as friends with whom to share their own lives and interests. Together they participated in sports activities and spectator events; a student or two would often accompany them during visits to offices at the graduate school; various teenaged "friends" were included among guests from many walks of life who attended weekend parties given by the program participants.

The men sought to know their students well because they valued them as people and also because they felt integrating the work of the school with the patterns of each person's *total* experience was most important. They saw the traditional school program as counterproductive in this necessary process of integration.

In public school programs, the three prospective teachers not only saw a schism created between the student's academic life and the one he knew on the street, but they also observed that the student's in-school involvements were being artificially segmented. A separation of the disciplines into discreet curricular areas did not reflect the true nature of knowledge, the trio felt; certainly it did not reflect accurately the context in which knowledge and skills were needed if one was to survive within a competitive but interdependent society. The participants wanted to show young people how they could *use* newly learned skills and to help them gain insight into their own potential for dignity in relation to the real world.

Eagerness to work closely with students sustained the participants during their intensive in-school experiences throughout the year. During this time they grew extremely critical of traditional secondary school programs. The process of examining prevailing practices developed in them the "desire" Dewey regarded as prerequisite to goal setting[1]:

We wanted to implement an educational approach which had as its basis the interrelatedness of academic disciplines. Through art we hoped to teach math; through discussions of personal problems, English; through the teaching of practical techniques of getting a job, writing skills.

The program they put together was intended to do these things by stimulating student involvement in activities that were organically related to community life.

Clive, Stu, and Ben developed a program that was keyed to the concepts of "practicality and relevance." The goals they established stressed the importance of "bridging the gap between school and community" and of enabling each student to express personal needs, clarify values, create original solutions to problems, and expand awareness by experiencing new ideas and environments. The three hoped to promote positive self-concepts and to increase the confidence of their students. They came to regard a program of meaningful work experience as the means by which the minischool's goals might be met. They recognized, however, that if they were to maximize success and minimize failure for their students, there would have to be opportunity for hidden talents to be discovered and for fleeting expressions of need and interest to be identified, acknowledged, and encouraged. Stu, Ben, and Clive perceived that flexibility would be the pivot upon which a successful program depended—that is, flexibility in their own teaching processes as well as in the curriculum. The program of work experience they developed was geared for flexibility so that it might be related to students' lives in ways the students would regard as immediately useful.

The creators of the Urban Studies Workshop did not regard their program as completely original in design. The summer program they eventually offered to young people was, they acknowledged, a composite of many approaches to learning. While some of these had been suggested by their own academic studies during the year, others they attributed to private and alternative school programs they had visited. They acknowledged that even some public school classrooms had suggested valuable ideas and techniques. Most important, however, were the wellsprings of dissatisfaction that arose from their own pasts. A flood of memories seemed to fill the reservoir of desire from which they drew sustenance for their commitment to change.

We, ourselves, had so many times experienced in our public school education and afterwards in college the boredom and apathy that results in a teacher-centered or subject-centered curriculum. The frustration and repugnance brought about in recalling these facts became even more intense as we made recent observations in a number of public schools. So often we observed the typical classroom of 30 or 40 students sitting in cramped desks, aligned in tight rows, all of which are faced toward the blackboard in the front of the room. There, next to the blackboard, sometimes writing on it, stands the teacher giving us the oration for the day. And, unattentively, sit the students who on a lucky day may get a word in edgewise. We promised ourselves that at Urban Studies Workshop this would never be the case.

The participants attributed the alternative approach they proposed to a post-World War II thrust toward vocational education.[2] In examining the post-war period, Clive, Ben, and Stu discovered a model that emphasized the value of personal work experience within the community—that is, "active and creative achievements as well as an adjustment to existing conditions." The three found such an emphasis grossly lacking in the thrust of public education during the sixties. Correspondingly, they observed that the education of this period "denied the student an important learning experience from which he could gain a sense of personal worth." They felt that both the individual student and the society had suffered through such denial: Students were diminished and brutalized, and while an uneasy decade had ended, educational processes had perpetuated the problems that characterized it.

An exception among programs the participants found in public school situations was one they observed during a trip to the San Francisco area. Among the places they visited was an experimental high school, where they saw in action a social science course with a community fieldwork component that involved the students during school hours. The three were impressed and thus made the first specific decision that shaped their minischool's curriculum: They would involve the students in community work experiences that they could bring back into the classroom for analysis and discussion. The curriculum content that eventually emerged was an outgrowth of this decision. The students would engage in, analyze, and research the urban environment in which they lived.

During the spring, Stu had become involved in a tutorial program for juvenile delinquents that was sponsored by an agency in an adjacent county. This affiliation resulted in an offer to the participants of a site for the minischool project—one that would include materials and a student group. However, the three minischool planners turned down the offer when they considered the advantages of working with students they knew and within a community where they were known.

At the same time that they explored possible funding sources for an afternoon work program, the three participants canvassed the community for a minischool site. One at an enclosed shopping center, and another at an abandoned town hall were unacceptable because of inaccessibility to their prospective students.

Hoping to get information about community projects in which their students might work, the three men went to the office of a neighborhood service center located on the grounds of a community church. They had heard that work programs were federally funded through this office. When they mentioned their need for a school site, the participants were referred to the church's pastor who offered them use of two large rooms *and* the sanctuary. The men accepted immediately. Later they noted that the spirit of hospitality and trust in which the offer was made had a significant effect upon the educational climate they were able to establish in the days to follow. It also encouraged them in a difficult undertaking.

The breadth of the work experience program they envisioned required that Ben, Clive, and Stu spread word of their impending project among many people in the community. In an all-out promotional effort they entered into discussions with persons filling a variety of roles and holding various attitudes. While most were sympathetic to the project's purposes as the three described these the response was not uniformly positive, and the participants experienced rejection along with frustration and disappointment. They began to doubt whether a business and civic community could be persuaded of the worth of such an endeavor and contribute to its support.

Obtaining summer jobs for their students was one thing; it was quite another to line up employment opportunities offering a chance for "meaningful" work experience—that is, job slots that bore a direct relationship to the objectives of the program. The three prospective teachers wanted their minischool students to learn skills and information that would benefit them in the future, and they submitted a course of study in which these objectives were indicated to the school district. An accompanying curriculum outline revealed the extent of their ambition.

They sought and ultimately obtained the accreditation by which their students could receive high school credit for participation in the Urban Studies Workshop. Each student would receive ten units of social science credit that could be applied toward graduation. Most students recognized the value of a high school diploma since employment and economic independence were matters of primary concern to the youths.

Stu, Ben, and Clive planned that their students would work in various city and county agencies in the afternoons. They hoped to sensitize each student to the "factors and processes he will face in his work that will provide him with valuable data in observing and understanding the community in which he is working and his agency's relationship to it." Correlated with this work experience thrust were curricular components stressing communications and interpersonal relations, urban theory and contemporary problems, and research methods for examining the processes and situations in which the students would be involved. Literature and field trips were expected to extend and define the students' experiences while casting them into broader perspective. They wanted their students to become aware of the basic interdependency among individuals and social institutions and to realize that just as they each had an investment in this relationship, they were important to it.

The description of their planned program made clear that Clive, Stu, and Ben placed as much emphasis upon process as upon content, which indeed they found difficult to separate in their dealings with students. They wanted "to come across as humanly as possible," and their primary goals stressed the importance of students' *personal* values and their finding opportunities to express *personal* ideas and needs in a *personal* way. Among personal needs, the three cited "the need for friendship and love; the need to be recognized and treated as a total person with unique ways of expressing one's self and one's talent." They wanted to expand each student's self-image and self-confidence—that is, to encourage students' growth by maximizing success in a range of experiences that would open up new possibilities for further growth. The three believed in the importance of achieving these goals without diminishing the value of students' lives outside the school environment.

The three recognized that their own flexibility would be the key element in determining whether or not their goals would be met, and they armed themselves with alternative strategies for fostering a student-centered curriculum: inquiry processes, simulation and gaming activities; and improvisation techniques such as role playing, sociodrama, and psychodrama. Through these means the participants hoped to promote greater awareness and understanding of different people in varying situations, and they hoped to lead students to self-discovery and self-direction.

The three minischool planners recognized the limitations of one six-week program toward the achievement of such goals. This time factor was another reason that the work experience program figured so importantly in their overall plan. Through it they hoped to provide students with employment that would continue after the closing of the minischool. Such employment would offer opportunity for income, increased independence, and self-respect. Additionally, by involving students and community persons with each other in mutually beneficial relationships, the minischool developers hoped to create a better understanding between the municipal agencies and the "disenchanted, and at times angry minority youth groups."

What Stu, Ben, and Clive discovered as they talked to agency people was that budgetary limitations stood as an impediment to implementation of the work experience aspect of the program. They decided to take the problem to the public with an appeal for support and funds. They wrote up a press release detailing their purposes and plans. They stressed the importance of the work experience as a problem focus for academic study with its potential for motivating school achievement and for fostering harmonious community relationships.

The existence of other summer work programs for youths that had already obtained commitments throughout the city meant that there was a dearth of job opportunities, however. Ultimately, the minischool planners obtained money from government-funded programs (Economic and Youth Opportunity Agency and Neighborhood Youth Corps) by which positions might be supported. They negotiated with each prospective employer for the creation of new jobs for their students. The tensions they experienced during this time arose from the pressure of working through political relationships and observing necessary protocol, while circumventing interdepartmental jealousies and bureaucratic red tape. They tried to keep all bases covered and worked out an informal system among themselves for attending to the multitude of details involved in launching their two-pronged program. While extremely time consuming, this approach enabled the three to design the kinds of positions in which they wanted to place their students.

Twenty-five students eventually worked at nine job sites. The students worked in emergency aid services, day care centers, and in departments of parks and recreation, fire, urban planning, redevelopment, computer programs, and human resources. Five served as staff assistants with the Urban Studies Workshop.

Some agencies were unable to participate in the program because they were saturated with students from other programs; others could not employ non-professionals because the work was hazardous or involved confidential casework. Still, Clive, Ben, and Stu felt gratified to have placed all their students in minimum-wage positions. They were especially pleased that for most students the employment opportunities would extend for four weeks after the minischool's program was terminated. They recognized the importance of this extension to the students. They also hoped that the young people would discover in their work experiences reasons for improving their basic skills and for developing their personal resources.

The participants felt that the site for the morning workshop offered many advantages. It was within walking distance of the neighborhoods served by the public school where they had worked with the secondary students during the spring. This accessibility was expected to encourage student participation as well as parent and community involvement. The grounds, parking lot, and commodious rooms permitted flexibility in the use of space. And while certain characteristics identified the church with institutional settings, it was free of the sterility associated with most public high schools. This aspect was important to the three minischool planners. They wanted the freedom to implement a non-traditional curriculum without procedural constraints. They wanted also to be free of the negativism implied in the usual school regulations: no smoking; no obscene language; closed campus, and so forth.

The pleasure the three planners felt at having found job slots and a location for their minischool was short-lived, however. The time required for making these arrangements and for establishing a curriculum as well as obtaining accreditation had taken a heavy toll. They also had been required to prepare their budget and to order and obtain the materials and supplies needed for implementation of their program. Additionally, they had to arrange for free lunches for all students. These tasks left little time for ensuring that the Urban Studies Workshop would be provisioned with the most important element in any school: the students.

Stu, Ben, and Clive planned for a low pupil-teacher ratio of around ten to one. They did not plan to register more than thirty students, and recruitment depended primarily upon their own personal contacts with students in the community's high schools. Additionally, the school principals were asked for recommendations, and the students they listed were contacted. The three planners were especially challenged by a list compiled by the principal of a continuation high school. None of the students named had been successful at regular high schools; all were completely "turned off" to school. Scanning the list of names, the three stated: "We knew if we could reach them and 'turn them on,' so to speak, it would be a positive result in terms of testing our educational design."

Essential to that design was a student group with a background of varied personal and cultural experiences. The participants had theorized that interaction among persons of diverse background during the afternoon work sessions would enrich the curriculum. They also regarded diverse personalities and lifestyles within the student body as a more important resource for the morning program than the books and materials they had ordered. While a group small enough to permit frequent and sustained pupil-teacher interaction was important, it was also essential that the group be large enough to accommodate a wide range of individual characteristics.

The three participants suffered some anxious moments on the Friday morning of their orientation session. Only five of the eighteen students they expected arrived within the first half-hour. Within an hour's time, nine were present. The three recognized that most youths interested in attending summer school had registered for the regular school district program and that this action had influenced their friends who were otherwise candidates for the Urban Studies Workshop program. The greatest problem, however, was that of overcoming the skepticism of young people who were "turned off" to anything resembling school.

Ben, Clive, and Stu were thus confronted with an important test of their flexibility on that first morning. They abandoned their planned format in order to concentrate upon winning the trust, confidence, and enthusiasm of those present. They continued in this same vein on Monday morning when four more students arrived:

We not only expected but insisted that our students express their feelings and reactions to the plans and ideas we disseminated. Naturally for many of our new students this was not an easy thing to do. They were used to receiving information or directions from a teacher without the chance to really question, reject, or alter it. We were, on the other hand, discussing plans and inviting students to make decisions concerning their implementation. In granting and affording this essential right we were fully aware of students' hesitancy and mistrust. We were working with, for the most part, a group of "failures" and "rejects" of the regular public schools, many of whom came from a local continuation program, and for obvious reasons felt threatened at this form of participation and involvement. We tried to work around these feelings by providing a warm, controlled environment where students aren't allowed to fail by not being put down for making mistakes. A student's thought or feelings whether agreed upon or not, were always accepted. Humor and informality permeated our gatherings with the intention of breaking down barriers and enhancing student involvement. We had the momentous task of trying to strengthen the confidence and self-image of our students and acquaint them again with the joy, curiosity, and will to learn.

The workshop students took more than two days to accept the responsibility and the opportunity their three teachers were offering them. A simulated communication experience was used to objectify the processes they were engaged in, and it enabled the young people to analyze and to evaluate these processes. The insights gained set the stage for total student involvement in two-way communication. Thus, the door for the students to criticize and evaluate their teachers was opened:

The first complaint came in the form of a written statement that was read to the class. The subject was the actions of two teachers who were felt to be treating certain students unfairly. What it boiled down to was the age-old problem of having certain pets and neglecting others in the process. The four-letter words included in the statement added dramatically to the accusation. The feelings of the accuser were, of course, well taken, and ways to resolve this problem were offered.

This is one example which developed that exemplifies the free, honest flow of communication and the integral part it played in the success of Urban Studies. Students began to feel important, realizing that what they had to say would be listened to and acknowledged. It was this freedom of expression consistent with our formal planned curriculum that was advertised around the community and that attracted to Urban Studies another 13 students which increased our student body to 27 by the second week of the program.

If the students' experience in schools had inhibited their willingness to express themselves freely, it had also alienated them from developing the means for effectively articulating their thoughts. Consonant with the assumption that the best way for students to develop skills was to involve them in activities requiring the employment of those skills, Clive, Ben, and Stu insisted that *all* participants, including themselves, write something every day. There were no guidelines and none of the external judgments that had made traditional writing exercises so repugnant to the young people. The first twenty minutes of each morning were scheduled for journal writing. Although the students at first resisted this structuring, their journals slowly began filling as a reservoir of trust was simultaneously built up within the peer group and between it and the teachers.

The journals were collected at the end of each week. By reading the entries, the "teachers" were able to gain insight into their students' feelings. Material regarded as too personal to be shared was labeled by the students with "Don't Read!"—an admonition the participants respected and observed.

While the participants regarded the communicative function as an important one, they valued it no less than providing students with the opportunity to learn more about themselves. And as students realized that they could write about anything of importance to themselves, they began to vent feelings and thoughts they had long hidden. Adolescent frustration and hostility emerged in words.

In My Room Crying

Oh! I hate them! I hate everything! I bet if I kill myself they'll be crying their stinken heads off . . . . They never let me go anywhere! "No, no, honey, you can't go because you haven't asked your daddy! Or, "No, you can't go because you'll come home too late." They've always got some kind of ---- to say.

The students began coming to school early in order to write more extensively. Some wrote in the evenings as well. Poetry, streams of consciousness, and dialogue began filling the pages and spilled over into moments of trustful confidentiality within the classroom. Sophisticated discussion ensued from issues of general concern that emerged. For example, turmoil and confusion with the issue of interracial dating led to socio- and psycho-dramatic explorations that formed the basis for subsequent discussions of related topics.

Recognizing that the written word was not the only legitimate means of communication, the students were encouraged to use many different vehicles for self-expression. The latent artistic talent of one student in particular flourished in this climate of acceptance. His work stimulated the graphic output of others, and before long the walls, ceilings, and doors of the minischool were covered with paintings, drawings, and sketches. Stu, Ben, and Clive noted that the student whose work fostered these efforts was a young man with a very poor public school record, and they observed that through the medium of art, he revealed intense thought and sensitivity:

His realistic works displayed love, knowledge, and pride of his ethnic culture and heritage. His more abstract creations displayed his deep-seated frustrations and hostility to people and institutions that have held him back so long.

From the beginning, the minischool's teachers sought to provide a classroom environment that challenged students to draw upon their own resources in the development of a climate for learning. While Stu, Ben, and Clive provided the materials, the art supplies, the visuals, the books, magazines, and newspapers, some stimulus problems, and guest resources, the student group itself "took off" and gave shape to the curriculum. The teachers' first assignment to the group illustrates this process and the way in which students' own resources were tapped.

As a way of getting acquainted with each other and in order to encourage self-exploration and knowledge, everyone, including the teachers, made individual collages based on the theme "Who Am I?" When the finished works were posted on the walls surrounding the room, an intense question and discussion period ensued. The group tried to decipher the content of each collage without knowing who was responsible for its creation:

After classroom investigation had been exhausted the creator would reveal himself and explain his collage and clarify misinterpretations. This format allowed for students to project themselves onto others' collages thus revealing themselves, and also served as a catalyst to get students to talk about their own work. . . . Also the important problem of miscommunication causing misunderstandings was treated. One by one we dealt with each collage, including those done by ourselves, realizing the uniquenesses of our group but also being aware of the common patterns and traits emerging. It would be these unique questions and commonalities that would serve as the focus of our curriculum.

Clive, Ben, and Stu recognized that the curriculum of the Urban Studies Workshop could not be separated from the personal concerns of students anymore than their behavior as teachers could be separated from their activities as counselors, friends, and confidants. As the level of trust rose between them and the students, personal crises were confided that revealed serious and bizarre problems. While acknowledging the importance of the counseling function to effective teaching, the three participants also recognized their own limitations and the dangers inherent in involving themselves too deeply in family and community affairs. They felt themselves fortunate that they were successful in referring the most serious "cases" to appropriate agencies for professional services and counseling.

The concerns and interests of students formed the basis for group work that centered about various urban issues. The groups formed in response to emerging interests so that by-and-large new groups formed each week. For example, one week a group of students addressed the topic of police-community relations while two others dealt with problems associated with education, including consumer education.

The three teachers wanted students to experience successful participation in the group process and to learn how they could effectively contribute in group situations. After groups read about and discussed their topics, they gave presentations to the entire student body. This format not only fostered cooperative planning and a sharing of information, but also gave students the experience of making public presentations. Some of these presentations stimulated further investigation of a topic and produced results that might not have occurred in a more tightly structured curriculum:

The presentation given by the police-community relations discussion group caused such wide interest that we immediately arranged a visit to the local police headquarters and also invited a number of ranking policemen to come to Urban Studies to talk about their work in the community. Although the visit to the Police Department was not particularly exciting for many of our students (for many, seeing the jail was old hat and recalled in their minds unpleasant experiences), it was the visit paid by a lieutenant in uniform to Urban Studies that proved to be the most interesting. Our students were primed and pent up with grievances and hostilities concerning anything that they referred to as the "pigs." They vented their feelings, holding nothing back. But the brave policeman visiting that morning handled each and every question and comment with coolness and directness. It was a day that provided learning on both sides of the fence and significantly it proved to our students that they could be acknowledged as people and listened to.

Another presentation dealt with the legal system and a group depicted, dramatically, a court room scene in which a poor man was being tried unjustly. Although the performance was a planned one, the dialogue was, for the most part, improvised and enabled the students to try on new roles and to experience new life situations. The involvement of the presenters in their roles captivated the audience group and stimulated a lengthy class discussion on the inadequacies of the judicial system and how it works specifically against the interest of the poor and the minorities:

The intensity of the issue grew to such an extent that we knew an actual trip to view a real court room session and also the chance to meet and speak to a lawyer and judge was a necessary step in the learning scheme. So with some difficulty we made arrangements to visit the courts and speak to a presiding judge. It proved to be a very fruitful and engrossing experience with our students anxiously asking questions and viewing the proceedings.

The minischool teachers recognized the importance of responding flexibly to the emergent interests of their students. The usual response was to arrange realistic encounters within the local community. However, they also recognized the limitations of that community in representing to students the multiple facets of a complex metropolitan environment. To bring the students into contact with such an environment required deliberate and detailed planning for trips to Los Angeles.

Such ventures were undertaken, and one of the most successful was a sixteen-hour exposure that put the entire student body in touch with various perspectives on the urban setting. Caravaning in several cars, the students traversed streets of the Los Angeles barrio noting the damage that had resulted from recent riots. They talked informally with the principals and student leaders of junior and senior high schools that were in summer session. The degradation and squalor that existed in large cities was observed during visits to housing projects located within "the concrete jungle." Following these stops, the students shopped in the central city, and then when they were tired, listened to soap box orators in a mid-city park.

While part of the group rode the bus to Watts to learn what many of its inhabitants endure as a matter of work-a-day routine, the rest of the group made the trip by car with two informative stops along the way. At the first of these, the students saw in operation a self-help, community-run endeavor that offered job training as a part of its business enterprise. At a central city community center they talked with exfelons who "spoke eloquently of their traumatic life experiences and what they were doing and hoped to do to ameliorate some of the discriminatory and oppressive conditions of our society."

The bus travelers eventually joined the others at the rendezvous point—the Watts Towers—after gaining some awareness of man's short-sightedness in the design of a system for mass transit. After also experiencing man's potential for vision as represented in the folk art of the towers, the group drove by freeway to the San Fernando Valley and the contrasting view offered by suburban life. In the valley they visited the clothing store of a young entrepreneur who explained how he started his business and what the running of it entailed.

The students enjoyed dinner in restaurants surrounding the Los Angeles campus of the University of California, which they toured before attending a nearby movie theater. There they viewed a documentary on the drug scene in Southern California that showed "the disaster in lives of real life dope addicts." Before they headed for home, the group cruised the Sunset Strip and walked around Hollywood Boulevard talking to the street people.

Such outings not only expanded the students' perceptions of the urban setting, but they also provided the Urban Studies group with a common bond of experience. This experience served to intensify the sense of community that was developing among them in spite of the diversity of work activities in which they were individually engaged on a daily basis.

These work activities, which were central to the concept of the Urban Studies Workshop program, proved to be the pivotal experiences that the minischool's planners intended: Almost every morning stories would come in about the afternoon work experiences and their effects on the students "in terms of morale, building confidence, and enhancing self-esteem, were extremely significant."

This is not to suggest that there were no problems, for there were. In assuming responsibility for arranging job slots for their students, the minischool teachers also felt the obligation to supervise the students in order to ensure that their performance met expectations held by employers. A number of changes were required in order to place students in situations appropriate to their abilities. The prospective teachers cited an instance in which one student with a low mathematical ability was placed in the city hall computer center. Recognizing that this student possessed exceptional clerical skills, the trio arranged to get her out of the computer center and behind a desk typing.

Another student excitedly took a position at a crisis intervention counseling center and then found herself washing dishes and sweeping floors when the participants had expected that she would take part in learning about the dynamics of the organization:

She brought her complaints to us and we immediately brought our dismay to the attention of the center's staff. Following this meeting, the girl was assigned to phones answering "hot line" calls. By doing this she was clearly learning a skill while serving a useful function. Another one of our students at the center became so involved and excited about her work that she persuaded her mother to volunteer at the crisis center.

Not all problems were so easily resolved, however. One young male student, who the participants described as "intelligent, proud, lazy, and hostile," was placed in four different jobs before one was found that sustained his interest and enabled him to function effectively. While such instances admittedly tried the patience of the minischool's teachers, there was a note of triumph as well as pride in their comment that "we never gave up on him."

Persistence and no little persuasiveness were required of the participants to locate twenty-eight teenagers in "meaningful," paying jobs throughout the community. The positions they filled ranged from telephone operator to an apprenticeship with the fire department:

We had six of our students working for City Hall in city planning and redevelopment. They were doing an assortment of things from performing clerical tasks to bookkeeping to actual involvement in map making and census taking. They would often bring in their work in the mornings and explain some of the future plans that were being considered for the city and some of the actual schemes that were going to be implemented. Toward the end of the summer they invited their supervisors to Urban Studies to present and explain in further detail some of the happenings in city planning and redevelopment. They brought slides and brochures and spent two hours giving us a very interesting look at the historical development of the city and the direction it would be heading in the future.

Ben, Clive, and Stu felt that the opportunities the Urban Studies Workshop offered its students also provided them with hope that the future they were headed for would be better than the past most of them had known. They observed that the results of the workshop "could never be measured in terms of improved reading scores or knowledge gained about the urban scene." They believed that their minischool's students articulated these outcomes when explaining the creations they made that were intended to represent their feelings about Urban Studies and their summer experience:

We put out an assortment of materials including paints, chalk, cardboard, styrofoam, etc., and said tell us what Urban Studies Workshop means to you. They said in many ways that it meant love, freedom, awareness, beauty, and determination. Personally we like to believe that Urban Studies more than anything else provided, through a multitude of experiences, the chance for people to relate honestly and humanely to themselves and others around them.

That the Urban Studies Workshop offered them such a chance was expressed in writing by some of the students. One of them wrote that "at urban studies, to me a teacher who cares about my whole life is more of a friend of whom I can relate much better to and feel at ease with when he tries to teach me." Another wrote, "I wish school could only be as good. I'll tell you something, if school was this way a lot more people would like it. And I bet a lot more people would learn more."

**Part IV
Perspectives on Schoolmaking**

12

Looking Back

The global differences that distinguished the minischools were evident to the most casual observer. Even those projects intended to serve similar populations were notable and instructive in their contrasting elements. The differences were apparent even to the participants themselves when their minischools joined in common activities such as a trip to a California mission. Victor and his associates, operating a more traditionally structured program, regarded Maxine's and Helga's informally organized group as generally disorderly and disrespectful. On the other hand, Helga and Maxine found Victor too controlling with his children. Such opportunities for the participants to make direct comparisons were infrequent, however, as cooperative planning between minischools was rare.

At the conclusion of the minischools, the participants were asked immediately to evaluate their experiences by answering the following questions:

What are the problems you encountered in your minischool?

With what did you feel you were most effective in your minischool?

If you were starting a new minischool what would you change?

What did you learn about students?

What did you feel you needed to make you a more effective teacher?

Five years later, after varied teaching experiences, the participants were asked to review the influence of minischools upon their subsequent professional behavior. Specifically, the survey inquired:

How did the minischool help you to become a teacher?

What did you learn from "doing" a minischool that you could not learn elsewhere?

In 1971, at the summer's conclusion, the problems that the participants reported encountering centered around personnel, pupil characteristics, lack of time, and insufficient preparation. The staff difficulties involved job assignments and delegation of roles. Tensions arose as a result of differences in goals, methods, and philosophies of education. Some who worked in groups saw a need for an elected "director" of their minischool. Some of the minischool students had overwhelming personal problems and some were disruptive. In addition, a high turnover in students made continuity difficult, and because the minischools

139

were short-lived, the participants found getting children involved in new and different activities difficult. There was not enough time for gradualism, for developing goals, for preparing helpers, or for planning lessons. Too much time was spent on logistical detail.

The participants regretted not having a greater fund of information—that is, information about the situations they entered, about organizational possibilities, and about the division of responsibility for teaching and learning. They stated that they did not feel sufficiently prepared to work with unmotivated students. They wished they had had more opportunities for realistic talks with open teachers about the problems involved in "free" classrooms. Finding and maintaining an optimum balance between openness and traditionalism was a continuing concern.

In spite of the problems the participants experienced and the deficiencies highlighted in their reports, they felt good about many things they saw as contributing to their minischools' effectiveness. Among these was the creation of a comfortable and stimulating environment in which children were able to interact in small groups. Students were eased into experiences at which they could succeed without the pressure to "cover material." Reading was enjoyed as an integral part of relaxed, unhurried activities.

The participants attributed much of the success of both students and minischools to the respectful acceptance of cultural difference that was manifested in the programs they designed and implemented. Spanish-English bilingualism and "Chicanoism," for example, characterized aspects of three different minischool programs. Environmental "openness" was valued for its message to children that the classroom was theirs to organize, control, and keep up; by choosing activities as well as "where" and "when" they would take place, the children were learning to assume responsibility for outcomes.

More advanced planning with more precise goals and more potential activities on hand were the principal changes that the participants regarded as necessary. Other suggestions for improvement included more individualized learning for specific needs, a stable group of students, and an understanding among staff about what constituted undesirable behavior. They recognized the usefulness of staffing the minischools in teams. They also saw a need for increased resources, including more money for educational games, materials, and field trips, and for air conditioned classrooms. Some felt that instead of attending afternoon classes, the participants should be free to spend the time with the children and their families.

From their experiences, the minischool teachers felt they had learned a number of important things: that children can be creative when given a free and failure-proof environment; that they are open, eager, and ready to explore new areas; that they need to relate their own experience to what they are doing and are more interested if they can do so; and that children, being extremely perceptive, can learn in spite of the teacher. Some participants found that even the youngest can be quite responsible and that even second graders can be helpful with younger children. Others discovered what an extremely significant effect the home situation has on children's school work.

Almost all the participants regarded experience and patience as the qualities they needed in order to become more effective teachers. They recognized the importance of having access to an experienced person who could assist and support them while questioning their assumptions and procedures. They realized that they must increase their ability to assess children's educational needs and to use a variety of teaching strategies appropriately.

When contacted five years later after wide-ranging experiences in schools, the participants' comments were seasoned by time and distance. Aspects of the experience, which at the time were not considered crucial, took on new importance. Ben, Stu, and Clive were unanimous in commenting on the value of the experience they gained in planning the Urban Studies Workshop. Stu stated:

I feel that the most important thing I learned was the planning that goes into putting an educational program together—whether a school such as we did with the Urban Studies Workshop or the planning necessary in putting a lesson together. . . . The experience gave me increased organizational and coordinating abilities.

Clive's recollection centered upon "the need for constant curriculum planning—curriculum planning relevant to the area of study and the needs and concerns of the present society."

These minischool builders also commented upon the number of roles they had had to assume during the project. Stu cited those of teacher, counsellor, and administrator. Ben added curriculum developer, materials purchaser, and janitor.

The direct contact the preterns had with the community was something traditionally prepared teachers would probably not experience. Clive learned to deal with a "multi-ethnic and multi-cultural situation." Ben remembered the need to "relate to the community where the school was located." The establishment of a minischool required "community awareness, contacts and acceptance." The "politics of the community," Stu felt, "became a reality one had to contend with."

The minischool offered opportunities for the participants to be with adolescents in many different settings. They saw many aspects of their students that helped them to understand and work with the young people more effectively. Stu felt the experience allowed him ". . . to work with a small number of students in a human and decent way with the time to enjoy each other. This made me want to become a teacher."

The participants valued the freedom they were allowed in making decisions. Ben commented:

The minischool assignment gave me freedom, I realized, in comparison to the rigid structure of public education. A small minischool is not tied to the bureaucratic inefficiencies plaguing the massive public school education system.

Responsibility and accountability came with the freedom they experienced. The participants were highly visible in the community and open to community scrutiny. Stu reported:

We were forced to think for ourselves, get our own material together, develop our own curriculum and recruit our own students. We worked without a large bureaucracy supporting us. We were visible and couldn't hide from our responsibilities as teachers under layers of an organization. We were indeed independent and free . . . and with this freedom came the burden and glory of individual responsibility.

The Urban Studies Workshop clearly was unique in providing experiences Stu, Ben, and Clive would not have had otherwise. All three praised the project for its effect upon them. Clive wrote:

I don't think I could have gotten the scope of my minischool experience in any other situation. Granted I could have experienced present day concerns and problems (of classroom teachers) in "traditional" situations . . . . However, in no other situation would I have been able to organize a school of my particular desire with a curriculum fitted to my particular concept of relevancy. In other words, "doing" the minischool allowed me a particular freedom that I don't believe I could have found elsewhere.

Stu summarized his feelings by saying: "It allowed me to be creative. It allowed me to feel important. It allowed me to develop an idea and test it and to see it through." In Ben's estimation, the minischool was ". . . the most beneficial and exciting experience I have had . . . [It] helped in developing my . . . *resourcefulness, creativity, dedication* and *discipline*."

The outcomes most valued from Helga's and Maxine's minischool, Ramona, were the crystallization of a philosophical orientation and the experience of implementing a "total" program. Helga stated that the minischool

. . . provided me with an opportunity to develop my philosophy, goals, curriculum and organizational structure from the very beginning. I was not required to fit into another teacher's organization or into a school's predetermined philosophy. Therefore I was much more aware of the underlying premises of the public school where I was hired, and consequently more able to resist or circumvent the ones I didn't like. . . .

She described her philosophy of education as "child centered" and felt it compelled her to "individualize" her methodology:

I've never adjusted well to static grouping. . . . One of the hardest things even now for me to do as a teacher is to decide what is to be taught and why it should be taught. Luckily, the minischool gave us practice in that skill. In this way I don't feel like I have to follow the decisions of others but can exercise my own discretion in choosing curriculum.

Maxine reported that the minischool enabled her to pursue an ideal. It gave her the opportunity to ". . . teach exactly what I wanted, to follow the theories that we had been taught, and all this before having been formed by the 'system'."

Because of their close relationship with the parents of their children, the Ramona minischool taught the two the importance of working closely with families and gave them experience with the Mexican-American culture. Maxine noted:

The opportunity for parent contact is not available in most (any other) education program before becoming a teacher. The minischool gave me experience and confidence in dealing with parents.

Helga added that since the minischool planning necessitated working directly with parents, it allowed her to realize the importance of parental support:

The parents' attitudes toward the school is one of the most important influences on whether or not a child succeeds in school. The experience I gained in working with parents during the minischool has been very valuable to me ever since.

That summer also taught the participants to "interface with the system." Helga reflected that she had had a chance to practice negotiation skills when she and Maxine had to confront the staff of the local public school. The experience also developed positive attitudes toward children. Maxine felt she was more able to enjoy the students as individuals and to try to understand the ones with which she was having trouble because she did not have to send home traditional reports in the form of grades.

"Scrounging" was a skill that both participants felt had been sharpened by their experience. They talked about having to learn to be resourceful since they had to set up their school "from scratch." Maxine observed that the minischool ". . . taught me how much a teacher can do with limited resources." On the other hand, having a small amount of money to spend made them feel that they had control over their curriculum.

Maxine felt that as the benefits of freedom of choice were extended to her, she was helped to learn their value: "The minischool gave us a chance for experimentation that is not possible in other areas. We could fail and not be judged. We could succeed and be praised." They were given the autonomy, she stated, to determine objectives and to choose evaluation strategies without pressures from their superiors. This experience, Maxine felt, could not be found in other programs and it was important to her development as a teacher.

Helga felt that she would not have acquired such skills and attitudes in a regular student teaching assignment: "Maybe, but probably not. . . . In fact I might have been suppressed or unsuccessful in a regular student teaching assignment." Helga regretted, however, that the experience had not helped her learn the "basic teaching skills." She attributed this deficiency to Ramona's short duration. As a result, she felt that while her "heart and mind were in the right place," her first public school class "really had a lousy educational experience." Through job experience, she has acquired these skills. She has also found that the philosophy and goals she formulated during that summer are still valid. She reported that the opportunity to learn as she did "prior to receiving a class of 30 to 35 students" prevented her from inflicting "gross damage" upon her first group of charges.

The reactions of its founders to La Escuelita were different than those of other schoolmakers toward their minischools. Pressures, conflicts, and frantic preparation appeared to have affected Victor's, Mia's, Flora's, and Sylvia's attitudes about it and what they derived from it. Mia reported that first-time teaching is an all-consuming, emotional, mental, and physical experience. In addition, she felt that the interns were "billed as exceptional, super people" and that this image built up extraordinary pressures upon them. Those pressures impeded efforts within the minischool, Mia reported.

Mia's experience during the years since the minischool summer had taught her that "teaching is murder." She said, "Six weeks wasn't enough time to assess and place the children in a strong language arts and math program. This was one of our main goals at La Escuelita. In retrospect, it was weak."

Sylvia, too, was uncomfortable with La Escuelita but for other reasons. She felt "alien" to what was going on when she was part of the project and later reflected upon the source of her feelings:

I functioned as an aide, not as a teacher. I had little input into the school. . . . My limited participation was not due to the other "teachers" but rather my own apprehensions about asserting my opinions about what was appropriate to a culture that wasn't my own.

She felt that she (and the others) mistakenly saw the children as "Chicanos" and not as "students" and that this was a shortcoming of this particular minischool. However, the situation ultimately forced her to deal with issues of ethnicity and education. Regretfully, she revealed that she could have learned more from her fellow "teachers" if she had been willing to openly question what they were doing. The experience was not lost, however:

I have never duplicated anything that was done at the minischool in my own teaching—so in some ways it helped me identify my own style of teaching by seeing what I was uncomfortable with in the classroom and with co-workers.

Victor also felt that the minischool experience had shortcomings. Some he attributed to the lack of appropriate "traditional" preparation during the previous year. He regretted not having seen examples after which he could model his program. He commented that the season and the environment worked against them. "Children are not that 'gung ho' during the summer," Victor noted. He observed that the classroom they selected was less than ideal in the hot summer weather.

La Escuelita allowed the group to "do our thing" in spite of the many difficulties. All the participants brought with them knowledge from personal experience as well as strategies they "picked up" by visiting schools during the academic year. Victor felt that their program was unique. He observed that it was "years" before the same school district instituted bilingual programs.

From the program, Victor learned that "it's harder than hell to get something like that put together. Not only in your teaching resources, but also to get permission to hold the school and all the rigamarole . . . the bureaucracy that you have to deal with, the city, school districts, and so forth."

In spite of the complexities involved in launching a minischool program, Flora saw that the benefits of a small, intimate program made their efforts worthwhile:

The minischool helped me become a teacher in that it allowed direct contact with parents and students. . . . The small group setting enabled me to work with each student on a personal level . . . thus developing teaching skills not normally defined in teaching manuals.

Like the others Flora felt, "Doing a minischool afforded me the flexibility to experiment with teaching methods and develop curriculum not normally dealt with in conventional teacher training programs."

The participants in Las Palmas felt strongly that *they* had gained professionally from the opportunity to participate in an open-ended but "safe" learning situation. Tina stated:

The minischool forced me to deal with all aspects of teaching without a "master" teacher to influence my choices. I made my own mistakes and learned from them. There were no expectations about what was going to happen in the minischool, except that it be good! Therefore we thought through each problem of curriculum, organization, etc., and solved each according to what we collectively thought was best for the children and for the program. . . . The minischool was a safe place to try out ideas—the presence of the other teachers was reassuring—if one of us bombed, someone else could pick up the pieces.

Tina felt that the minischool summer had helped her to develop her own style:

Through experimentation, I learned what felt right to me, what my own style was, to what extent I needed to direct activities, the way I best related to children—or at least, began to learn these things. This all led to a sense of being comfortable with the role of "teacher."

Assuming the teacher's role was also very important to Boyd. He was aware that new teachers trained in traditional programs were usually socialized quickly into the school system and felt that he had more freedom to choose to behave nontraditionally:

There is a socialization of new teachers; there are rites and rituals; there are expectations. Preopening potlucks, meeting the Board, taking a tour of the town with the principal, being called a "student teacher," meeting the new teachers, paying in the Sunshine Fund, and learning a bit about Tupperware—this is the weight of a strong process.

Boyd found the fact that the minischools involved no preconceived role expectations was significant. Activities and relationships seemed to develop naturally:

We were the minischool. Having taught before ultimately becoming a member of the priesthood helped me to have a different relationship with the kids. I remember that on Friday of the first week we had a play, people came, and it was working.

Because the minischools were responsive, parent involvement took on a greater importance than it normally would for a traditional student teacher. Tina reported:

I learned the value of parent involvement. Our aide not only assisted us, but she paved the way for our acceptance in the community, helped us align ourselves with the children, and gave us a sense of how we were being received . . . another important goal that I carried into teaching.

Gail stated that she ". . . learned the value and importance of parental support and saw that when parents are included in the celebrations, and they see their children as involved and competent members of the group, they will give that important support." The minischool was a perfect vehicle for that lesson because ". . . the parents were right there and their support was based strictly on what *we* had done. It was not public school connected in any way."

The preterns also had to relate to other groups in the community:

We convinced some reluctant community leaders to OK our school; we constantly informed the whole community of our progress through a daily paper and weekly celebrations. We ended after six weeks with a carnival and had a great turnout. That seems a better crack at accountability than these pro-forma behavioral objectives, standardized testing, etc.

The preterns learned to interact with the children in unique ways. Tina found that "active, involved children are not generally a problem. That knowledge has helped me take all the burden of behavior off the child and place it partly on my shoulders."

Of course there was the advantage that the children chose to be there, which is not the case in public schools. "I felt successful, validated, encouraged—especially when minority administrators marvelled at the success of a 'non-traditional' project," said Tina; "It was a sense of achievement that helped in job interviews and in the frightening beginning days of teaching. We all need lots more of that sense."

Tina felt this sense of *personal* accomplishment validated the minischools:

The value of "doing" can't be overstated. It was invaluable. The context doesn't compare with student teaching, where roles are already defined, where the full responsibility lies with the teacher, where you're faced with a full class of kids within a context determined by someone else's personality. . . . The more "doing" in a safe place, the better.

The minischools, however, were not activities for activities' sake. They had a philosophy; they had goals; they had a purpose:

I learned the value of some overall goals and ideas, and of a structure designed to accomplish those goals. It makes the day-to-day activities more meaningful and directed. Again, I don't think that could have been accomplished in a situation other than the minischool, where we had full control of the six-week program and were not sidetracked with requirements. We could concentrate on seeing our ideas through.

As a result of the minischools Gail has remained an experimenter:

Schools of course have many expectations of their teachers, but I have continued that valuable process of experimenting, rather than making automatic "teacher" responses to various situations.

Cal's minischool was the result of an enterprise already in process. He perceived his endeavor as significantly different from that of the others. Since he was interested in providing a long-term stable contribution to the community, he elected to become part of the Black School that had operated on Saturdays throughout the year. His prior experiences with schools, he felt, helped him to recognize some of the pitfalls of institutionalized education.

The children at the Black School ranged in age from five to eighteen. Cal felt that because of this age range he was able to obtain a longitudinal view of child development and to "observe and interpret" student behavior from this perspective. This ability helped him to bring an understanding of children to his years of teaching. It also made him aware of the inadequacy of traditional curriculum in meeting the developmental needs of the young.

Cal valued most, from his experience, the opportunity he had to informally relate to students:

At the Black School, we were on a first-name basis. We had a very informal atmosphere. I was personally able to function better in this type of situation as opposed to the formal situations of the last four years.

Since the minischool, Cal has continued to meet with students at his home at least once a month and to take them to nonschool events. He pointed out that since his informal relationship with students runs contrary to the expectations of other teachers with whom he works, it has ". . . perhaps been detrimental to me as a public school teacher." Although he has tried to reeducate the thinking of other faculty members, he reports that he has not succeeded.

Freddi, in reflecting upon her experience, recalled that the abstract concepts she had been learning became realities under the day-to-day minischool challenge. She knew intellectually that each child grows at a different rate but *experienced* it in working in her minischool. She discovered also that "artificial barriers between grade levels" are meaningless. Because she observed children learning in different ways, she realized that some quickly grasp meaning and others progress more slowly, that she had to provide a variety of learning opportunities for her children, and that each child needed "appropriate" experiences. The minischool also taught her that all the staff should work cooperatively in planning programs for individual children. In summing up her feelings, she said:

Specifically in dealing with the minischool, I discovered the importance of studying the environment of the students including neighborhood, parents and economic factors. This of course was of great assistance in planning curriculum. This also provided me some insight as to what would help or hinder the goals and objectives planned for the students.

In summary, fourteen program participants established, "ran," and disbanded six minischools during the summer of 1971. While they developed each minischool in response to local needs and with the intention that it "belong" to the community in which it was located, the participants themselves maintained a proprietary perspective toward their little schools.

From their minischool endeavors, the schoolmakers gained a sense of personal achievement. Because the opportunities were open ended, learning experiences were malleable. In the process of shaping these for their charges, the participants were able to construct and reconstruct their own philosophies, apply and test the theories they had learned, define and redefine their roles. They were able to relate to children in a way very different from that of teachers in the public schools. They were able to approach problems of teaching and learning experimentally because just as there were no externally imposed demands, they would not be called to account according to someone else's standards. They felt safe from arbitrary judgment, and this sense of safety gave them a feeling of freedom that went beyond exemption from mandate. This is not to say that the participants did not hold themselves accountable, because they did. They took their mission most seriously. But they were the ones who established the criteria by which the success or failure of their work might be determined. All of them expressed a profound desire to succeed. All experienced a measure of success.

In two-thirds of the minischools, "success" was a shared achievement. The team effort was a new experience for some of the participants. Most recognized in it a source of mutual support, both emotionally and in terms of complementarity of function. They valued this experience; they attributed to it the ability to assume responsibility for which in many ways they had not been fully prepared. They all recognized the need for information and strategies related to the teaching of "basic skills." Their comments with regard to accomplishments in their minischools did not include expressions of complacency with regard to the craft of instruction.

Although schoolmaking was central to the concept of the program and its most visible aspect with regard to assessment, it was not the total program. Academic course work and field activities preceded the minischool summer and a year of supervised internship teaching followed it. All of these were expected to have increased its meaning. To place the minischool experience within the larger context, the initial questions asked of participants related to their original expectations and the effectiveness of the entire program.

The survey solicited an update of their activities since the minischool summer. It sought a personal and retrospective analysis of the program and inquired about the program's effectiveness in relation to individual goals. To remind them of their original expectations, their personal statements written at the time of application were enclosed with the mailed survey questionnaire.

A central purpose of the inquiry was to assess the participants' effectiveness as the result of the program. Although follow-up telephone calls were necessary in some cases, ultimately the entire group responded in writing, or orally on the blank tapes that were provided, or through personal interviews. The questions asked were open ended in nature in order to limit the researchers' control over responses.[1] Subjects discussed included goal congruence, goal achievement, evolution of purpose, preparation in relation to other programs, and the power of the program to prepare "different" kinds of teachers. In addition, their reports on career patterns over the last five years enabled the investigators to place the participants' sentiments in a situational context.

After a preliminary review of the data, the investigators felt eliciting supplementary information about the minischools was necessary, and a second questionnaire was therefore constructed and distributed. All of the participants responded; these data have been reported in the first part of this chapter.

Through written and oral answers to open-ended questions, the participants showed that they had reflected on the program and their hopes for it. None felt that their purposes had been automatically fulfilled as a result of the program. Although their retrospections revealed that as a group they were as diverse in their specific objectives as they had been when they were together in the program, they nonetheless shared a common perspective toward it.

Many of the participants suggested that by promoting "the development of insight," the program had functioned to affirm, to clarify, and to extend their goals. Helga commented that the program strengthened her belief in individualization and in the importance of choice for children. Flora noted that the program ". . . helped me verbalize my goals more effectively and enabled me to broaden my exposure to problem areas." However, in her further comments, she seemed to question the importance of this result. "*Sensitivity* is the key in teaching!" she declared. Since she found the academic work dulling to her sensitivity, she felt better prepared to teach *before* she embarked upon her studies. The participant who left the program before implementing the minischool she had helped to plan stated that the program had shed light on what she was *not* suited to do.

Another group felt that goals were very clear right from the outset. By and large, this group was composed of the minority participants who in 1970-71 were highly critical of the program. With Flora, they saw the program's *academic* offerings as irrelevant to the program's stated purpose. In 1975-76, however, their sentiments had changed. They now regarded the goals of the program as simplistic in the light of social complexities. No longer was all criticism leveled at the means of attaining goals; the goals themselves were seen as unrealistic.

This is not to say that after five years the academic content escaped the type of denunciation that characterized the sixties. The program's relevance as well as its sufficiency and its effectiveness continued to come under attack. One participant questioned the program's relevance to their future lives: "Our training was largely irrelevant to what we grew to be." Another questioned its relevance to their pasts. Maria wondered about the program's relationship to a cultural history from which her identity emerged: "Being a minority individual, I felt that there was so much that wasn't being said . . . especially for those who were going to be working with Mexican-American children and parents."

Mia's view of the program after five years was similar to what she expressed during the first year of her participation in it; this perspective was characteristic of many of her peers at that time also. Most came to the program with goals that were very specific. They were committed to improving educational circumstances for a particular racial or cultural subgroup of society or were interested primarily in the problems associated with teaching students within a particular age group. For some of these persons, the program seemed too diffuse. They regarded the help they received as poorly suited for achievement of their goals. The questions they asked were often rhetorical in nature and reflected a single purpose to which the program seemed unresponsive and the instructors insensitive. These participants sought precise skills for solving specific problems. If an activity did not address their specific concerns, it was regarded as irrelevant or ineffective.

After five years of work in school settings, however, even the two most "militant" minorities in the group seemed less eager to criticize the program for unachieved objectives; instead, they questioned their own goals as being "naive" or "idealistic." Cal and Victor saw the program as "helping." They did not regard its impact as impressive. Cal said that perhaps the program helped him to "make dents" in an ineffective system that is fairly impervious to change—especially change from the inside; Victor commented that a classroom teacher "cannot do that much change . . . because if he tries to change very much, or if he tries to change the system in any way . . . he'll get burnt, you know!"

Sylvia, too, acknowledged that ". . . my goals were pretty high-flying." She commented that for one person in a school district to aspire to make education "meaningful for all" was fairly unrealistic when one's school board "has decided pretty much what is meaningful and what isn't." Unlike Cal and Victor, she has not modified her goals, however. While the program experience has not yet enabled her to accomplish her goals, she still believes that it will: "It taught me to hang in there. It gave me people for support that I know I can always turn to."

Gail said that for her the process of becoming a teacher was a continuing one. Helga also recognized that any expectations participants held for immediate results were unrealistically cast within a fanciful and surrealistic time frame. From the beginning, she showed interest in psychological and philosophical issues. She wrote that in the light of day-to-day experience, she continues to examine her choices among teaching methods and to study the relationship between freedom and responsibility in the options she offers to children.

The long-range view had also come to be accepted by Ben. To become a successful and effective teacher "takes more than a two-year program," he stated and observed that "It takes years!" Ben said that the program "served as a catalyst in promoting certain opportunities that I've had." These included his initial teaching position in a disadvantaged area.

There were participants who expressed strong negative feelings about the value of the program in general. Flora declared that it was of limited value because of repetitious content and instructors who were insensitive to the needs of Chicano students. Courses taught by minority instructors were most influential, she said. While Helga expressed positive feelings toward a program that supported and reinforced her beliefs about the value of options in personalized learning, she did not think that she was given enough skills to be an effective teacher; neither did she feel that she was helped enough in understanding the children she was going to teach.

Although some took a censorious stance, after half a decade, many cited particular program experiences that contributed in an important way to their preparation. The opportunity to apply what they were learning was of critical importance. Stu observed that the program helped him get in touch with students by providing him with strategies he could apply at the local school level. Freddi commented that because of insights gained in the program, she was better prepared to help young people find their place in society at large as well as in their own communities. She regarded her training as "very valuable" since she learned to apply many of the theories discussed in her academic courses.

Boyd, too, expressed a particular interest in theoretical aspects of learning and development. He felt the program helped by building upon his understandings in these areas, particularly with regard to linguistics. Educational theory was especially important to Clive as a base for coping skills and hence for survival in the system. Clive attributed to the program his increased awareness of the need for community involvement and of the role "politics" plays in educational decision making. He placed high value on the opportunity for personal involvement in decision-making processes.

Like Clive, many participants valued the opportunity to consider alternatives and to make decisions. When asked what aspects of the program were most influential upon their subsequent professional behavior, they commented on the emphasis upon problem solving, which they attributed to the "Claremont philosophy." Again and again their responses gave evidence that they saw the need to probe beneath surface appearances. They questioned assumptions related to the learning process, to curriculum, and to relationships among ethnic groups. Maxine stated, "The program rid me of prejudice and helped me overcome a patronizing attitude. . . . It allowed me to criticize blacks and Chicanos as well as to be friends with them."

Maxine's comments suggest another aspect of the program reportedly valued by many of the participants: their association with each other. This outcome was unexpected, since during the program getting the participants to work together and to form a learning community was difficult. The survey revealed that after a period of germination, the exchange of ideas, opinions, and prejudices had borne fruit. Participants recalled the interactive process, while painful at the time, as being highly productive and of continuing importance. Although geographically scattered, most reported sustained contact with some of their fellows.

Predictably, however, the minischools were given a large measure of credit for the program's impact upon them as teachers. Since it was conceived before they were admitted to the program, the participants viewed the program preparatory to the minischools as "beyond their control." On the other hand, *they regarded the minischools as their own,* separate from the rest of their academic experiences and self-generated. This view was evident in the way they responded to the inquiries made to them about the effects of "the program" upon their professional behavior. Their initial responses dealt almost exclusively with their experiences during the academic year. Little was said about the minischools. Subsequently, when they were asked specifically about their summer experience, their comments were copious and revealed that the minischool experiences stood out in high relief as especially concrete and identifiable aspects of the program. Their reports focused upon how the minischools helped them to become teachers and what they had gained from their efforts.

Among benefits from minischools the participants mentioned the community involvement that was made possible by the projects, the perserverance developed in bringing the projects to fruition, as well as such managerial skills as budgeting and planning. Stu felt that by being given the chance to create a school curriculum, he had learned that things must often be done on one's own without the help of others. This theme of independence was echoed by Mia who felt that the minischool was a good experience because ". . . we chose our situation and it was our doing—our own students and everything." Boyd stated, "The minischool gave me great pride. I will always remember it as a good and successful venture. I frequently wonder why . . . everyday and every school is not mini."

13 Looking Around

Since 1972, the schoolmakers' careers have developed differently. One group has remained in teaching and appears to be oriented toward working directly with children. A second group has set its sights on affecting organizational structures by entering administration or by university teaching. Another group has left the public schools to work with young people in different settings. A few have left education all together.

Stu, Ben, and Clive have participated in a variety of professional activities since working together at the Urban Studies Workshop. After one year of teaching, Clive was offered a position as the acting black studies director at a nearby university. He resigned from his secondary school job teaching social studies in order to assume this position, which, as it turned out, only lasted one year. Since that time he has had difficulty reentering the public schools and has had to be satisfied with irregular teaching activities: substitute work in high schools, instructing extension courses for several colleges, and part-time involvement at a community college teaching Afro-American history and literature. He hopes to be able to return to full-time teaching when the economic situation becomes better and a person with an advanced degree is not considered overqualified and overpriced. Ultimately, Clive reports, "I hope to be either principal of a high school or an administrator in a community college district—positions where *I* can make some decisions." He thinks that a doctorate in Urban Education would be an asset toward achievement of his long-range goals.

In 1976 Stu and Ben were also found working outside the public schools, although both remained involved with education. After four years as a secondary teacher of mentally retarded youth to whom he taught creative writing, reading for enjoyment, and forestry, Stu became the associate director of an Upward Bound program. Federally funded and with headquarters on a college campus, the program brought adolescent youth to the campus for enriching activities. Stu always had a love of the outdoors and has worked to plan programs for young people at Yosemite National Park and other rural locations. Five years after the minischool ended, he was continuing his education toward a Ph.D. degree. Projecting another five years, Stu sees himself still working with youth—even going back into the classroom where he enjoyed a close relationship with the young people he taught. He muses, too, about going into private business in order to get enough capital to ". . . carry on the kind of educational and community work I want to be involved in." Stu states that despite roadblocks and the inadequacies of the educational system or

155

of the people within it, he will continue to be involved in education, wherever he might be.

Ben worked for three years as a junior high school teacher. During that time he directed his efforts toward helping disaffected youth return to the regular classroom. He organized "halfway" classes and was instrumental in getting other teachers involved. He mobilized community people as counselors to give the youngsters needed support, and for his efforts he was nominated by his district for a national award of recognition.

Ben ultimately realized that he had little impact on educational practice as long as he remained in the classroom: "My creative energies were not being channeled in the most effective way. . . . So I began to look in other places." He became the head of a juvenile diversion program that drew on over twenty agencies within the community. In 1975 he was accepted into an executive management doctoral program and anticipates that he will continue to work for "the betterment of people.'

The goals of La Escuelita participants have led them in different directions. Just as their minischool was differently oriented than the Urban Studies Workshop, the program participants who operated it had different career objectives. Sylvia, Flora, and Mia are still teaching in elementary schools. In nonschool hours, Sylvia has continued her commitment to helping handicapped children and adults. At a community college, she has conducted a "sensitivity class" for nonhandicapped people and has served on an advisory committee on problems of the handicapped. Mia and Flora are still concerned with curricular inclusion of the Mexican-American culture. This concern, which dominated Mia's bilingual-bicultural activities during her early classroom teaching and during a period as inservice consultant to a Follow-Through program, has broadened. When surveyed, Mia reported that she was working with native Americans and migrant families in a trilingual classroom. Flora, who was the oldest program participant, has also broadened her commitment. She advises "older" women who are returning to work or school and has gone back to school herself to get another master's degree—this time in guidance and counseling. "After several more years in the classroom, I *may* enter the field of counseling," she reported. When asked about future plans, all three expressed a vague feeling of dissatisfaction with what they were doing, but not a strong inclination to leave teaching.

Victor's career pattern differs markedly from the women with whom he worked. Although he has remained in the classroom as a bilingual teacher, he has become involved in political affairs as a member of the Association of Mexican-American Educators and has served as its vice president. He has returned to school for both his administrative certificate and the new California bilingual-bicultural credential. He sees himself working as a principal or in the directorship of a bilingual program in the near future, while taking steps toward ultimately achieving a superintendency. "A superintendent can do a lot to change the system," he observed. On the other hand, he added, "I might possibly have to get out of education in order to change it."

Helga and Maxine, the two Anglo women who founded Ramona, have maintained their commitment to the Mexican-American community. Because of Maxine's efforts, the school district, where she has taught both junior high and elementary classes, instituted a bilingual-bicultural program at both levels. In addition, she has published several articles in national magazines. Maxine plans to go back to school to begin a doctoral program aimed at preservice and in-service teacher preparation.

Helga teaches in a bilingual primary classroom. She dreams about opening a school of her own focused on the early years. Hoping to become still more active in bilingual programs, she plans to spend time in Mexico and to travel in South and Central America. When asked about the changes she has made since leaving the program, Helga replied, "I've been very quiet. It's taken me these five years to feel professionally competent and successful as a teacher. Now I can begin to open my mouth a little more."

Boyd and Gail, two of Las Palmas' founders, have since married one another. Both are still teaching, although Boyd has opted to work in a private alternative school in a black community. Their partner, Tina, concerned that she may have entered teaching because it was "a woman's field," has left it for the world of publishing:

One reason I needed to get out of teaching is because it's a real female job. It was really important to me to leave it for that reason . . . and to see if there was something else. I wanted to see if teaching was just something that I fell into because I was a woman and it was a woman's job. . . . In the end I think I'm going to find out that that was not at all the reason and that I am really a teacher and that I really do love it.

Gail has continued to be an upper grade teacher, but does not plan to teach indefinitely. With a perspective toward her female identity that differs from Tina's, Gail expects to leave teaching for a while to begin a family, and then ". . . I'll probably wind up working in some leftover poverty program using organizational skills that I am not using to any real advantage now." Gail has not been teaching in a low-income area, although she feels both her own orientation and the program readied her to do so.

Freddi, who set out to run Live Oak alone, continues to be independent. After one year in the primary grades of a school system near Claremont, Freddi moved to an agricultural center in California's central valley. She helped to develop a preschool program in her school district and became coordinator of the prekindergarten program. Her time was occupied with program writing, curriculum development, and staff training. Two years later she became a parent education resource teacher and in working primarily with parents taught them what they should expect of the schools and how they could help their children to get more out of the schooling experience. Through Freddi's efforts the district's parent education program was implemented.

In addition to her school district duties, Freddi also helped to train twenty-five high school and college students to become tutors who, in turn, worked with over 150 black elementary students. Additionally, she has taught a course in child growth and development at a community college. Freddi seeks to further develop her competence to work with students at the college level. She hopes to return to graduate school for a doctorate in teacher education.

Cal, also a loner, moved back to Virginia after he had completed the program. While continuing to teach sixth grade, he served as coordinator for a cultural arts center and as a musician. Five years after the minischool summer, Cal returned to California to begin a new career. He took a job as a hearing aid company sales representative where he still keeps in touch with children who have special needs:

Perhaps the easiest way to describe my five years of teaching is by saying "I have learned much more than I taught; I have received more than I gave. . . ." I knew positively three years ago that teaching was not what I should be doing. The problem was not that I wasn't a good teacher—I was an above (slightly) average teacher but I would never become a great teacher, by my standards.

The participants' pursuit of particular interests and concerns led some into political activity, others into program coordination and supervision within the schools, and still others into people-related work outside the schools. While also indicating wide-ranging interests, about half the group had taken steps to increase their professional capacities and credentials through further studies in higher education.

The group had been encouraged to look back and to evaluate their earlier preservice experience, especially their minischool experiences. They did so after five years of work in varied professional settings. Within each of these settings there were colleagues whose backgrounds and preparation contrasted markedly with their own. As the schoolmakers looked around them, they compared themselves with other teachers and assessed their own powers as teachers and innovators.

Many participants admitted to feeling "lost and unprepared" at first. But while they felt deficient in the "mechanics" of teaching in comparison with most of the teachers with whom they associated in school settings, they repeatedly commented on their own greater flexibility and openness. Stu felt that he was better able to improvise and to turn desperate and deteriorating situations into environments conducive to learning and that his training enabled him to "pull it off," or to come up with new ideas that were student centered. Ben, too, thought that the program equipped him with an effective way of relating to students. However, Ben said he had known some very effective traditionally prepared teachers who have the ability to communicate with students: "The *feeling* that you project is as important, if not more so, than the methodology you might use in working with kids." Still, he believes that "some of the new, more innovative methods that I was exposed to are, in the long run more positive and do more good for the kids who experience them."

Gail was one who confessed that the student-centered approach did not prepare her for her initial teaching experience and that she did not know how to ditto or how to give grades:

Traditionally-prepared teachers seem to slip into traditional methods without questioning anything. I tried everything and finally came up with what I feel are the best methods for me and for the kids. For example, at first I never considered starting from page one in a textbook, using prepared questions, etc. I preferred to be selective or sometimes not to teach from it at all. It was hard, and it's still going on, but it's been important in my forming a personal, well-thought out philosophy of teaching. I was determined not to be the kind of teacher that I knew about as a child and later as a visiting observer.

Clive said he felt better prepared than most of the traditionally trained teachers: "I was more aware of the need for community ties and involvement than they were." Although valuing his greater flexibility, he also regretted the lack of certainty that goes with it. Clive wrote that he envied traditionally prepared teachers' ability to "deal with the lack of reading and writing skills of the students." At the same time, however, he acknowledged the rigidity that characterized their methods.

Helga was glad she did not have to take most of the traditional classes since ". . . that's not the way I personally learn . . . I don't think I'd have made it," she confessed. But she said she did not feel better prepared as a result of the program's structure either; "maybe equally prepared in most ways," she said, but less well prepared in skill areas. She, like Sylvia, felt that she had not been given a tool kit of skills to use in each of the curriculum areas and that she did not have ways of diagnosing the status of children in relation to a predetermined sequence. Helga commented that she had become so suspicious of mass-produced materials that she shunned them even when their use might have been appropriate.

Like Helga, most of the participants felt that there was not enough attention given to "content" or what some called "the nuts and bolts" of teaching— the "how-to" or mechanical and technical aspects—particularly, they claimed, in the teaching of reading. Many mentioned the need for a competence they did not feel they possessed at the conclusion of the program. They regarded this deficiency as one that could have been remedied had they been taught specific "reading methods" in the mode of more traditional teacher preparation programs. Even as he expressed this opinion, however, Boyd admitted "I would have vigorously protested had they been required."

The implied conflict between Boyd's expressed need for "know-how" and the demand for freedom in which to find one's own answers and teaching style was expressed by former program participants time and again. It was expressed in a collision between what was identified as "the program philosophy" and the pragmatics of an anxiety-producing profession in which teacher control over behavior and outcomes are often more valued than the people involved. This conflict was frequently conceptualized by the program participants as strengths and weaknesses in "The Program" when it was compared with traditional programs of teacher preparation. Maxine's comments are representative:

The program formed my basic teaching philosophy. Rather than the traditional "textbook" work I have felt freer to use open-ended kinds of teaching experiences (for example, putting Goldilocks on trial for breaking and entering).

On the other hand, my lack of being able to identify problems . . . and have available answers made me feel unprepared. (How does one go about teaching division, anyway? I still have a difficult time when it's presented three different ways in textbooks and I don't know which is acceptable.)

Like Maxine, the participants overwhelmingly attributed to the program's influence their teaching philosophy and their own pedogogical strengths and weaknesses. Only one, Flora, said without qualification or elaboration that as a result of the program she did not see herself as a different kind of teacher—different, that is, than she might otherwise have been.

The importance of concrete experience, including what they had gained before entering the program, was always emphasized by the participants. A few regarded prior experience as *the most* influential element and declared that motivation comes from background, not from any program. Mia stated that what made a difference was not so much "preparation," but rather "upbringing . . . the fact that I am Mexican-American." She explained that she shares experiences with other Mexican-American teachers, children, and parents—experiences that are different from those of Anglo students and teachers. Since many commercial materials have become available, many teachers are able to work in bilingual education, she noted. However, she implied that their effectiveness may be questioned since "motivation comes from background, rather than a program. . . . The basic thing is that I am 'Mexican'."

Tina, too, regarded preparation as fairly meaningless. To Tina, however, what mattered was not *prior* experience but rather what came *after* the teacher preparation program. Tina referred to some of the "terrific teachers" she had encountered, all of whom were traditionally prepared:

I just think that it's what you do with it afterwards that makes the difference. . . . It's how you grow in the context. I'm not saying that programs don't have any effect, because I think they probably do . . . but in the end it's the person . . . it's an art and not a science.

She found generalizing about whether this art could be practiced in public school settings difficult to do, but thought it might be possible in some districts or schools. That depended on the climate of support and the people. They make the difference, she said.

Neither Boyd nor Freddi regarded themselves as "different," either, but in their comments they suggested that the kinds of teachers they turned out to be was more a function of personal characteristics than it was of the program's influences upon them. They indicated that the program had been personally compatible, however, because of the opportunities for interaction with persons of similar interest and concern. They felt that the program had developed in them an awareness of individual differences and of the need for alternative approaches to teaching and learning. They valued this philosophical emphasis in the program's content. They felt that the program, itself, was structured to reflect this emphasis. Boyd observed: "The program was quite flexible for me. Because I could pursue my interests, what I learned stands out as something I own. . . . It's mine."

Several, Tina among them, attributed the fact that they actually did become teachers to the existence of a supportive program that did not impose "the usual teacher education mush" upon them. Comments to this effect seemed to have more to do with the perceived existence of a permissive atmosphere and to the things they were *not* subjected to, than it did with positive influences toward being a quality teacher. For some, to teach at all meant to teach differently. The program enabled them to teach differently. Helga, with Tina, was not so sure that it had taught them to teach as well as they hoped to do.

Tina felt that the emphasis on experiential learning—while "very good because I learn by doing"—precluded the group's developing the theoretical understandings that were needed. She declared, "I missed that!" Her particular interest, which she shared with Helga, was in early childhood education. Both women would have liked to have gained control over "a real body of knowledge" in this area, and Tina wished she might have explored deeply into the arts as well. "It was just a question of we all didn't want the same things," she said. Tina felt that "an inordinate amount of time was spent in discussing whether or not we even had a right to be in the schools at all."

Since they all *had* been in the schools, most compared their own preparation with "regular" or "traditional" or "conventional" programs of teacher training. They looked at their teaching behavior and contrasted it with what they saw around them. While some were dissatisfied, others felt their own performance was superior to what it would have been without the support of the program. Sylvia observed that if she had gone through a regular program, she would probably just be one of those traditional classroom teachers ". . . being very bored, and I probably wouldn't still be there!" Stu credited the program with giving him important strategies and techniques—an expertise that paid off through "contacts" considered useful in moving him toward his goals.

Dominating many of the answers that were directly affirmative or were positive in tone was a program "philosophy," as identified by several respondents. This orientation seemed to set them off from other teachers. It helped them to relate education to a broader social context and suggested the importance of *flexibility* in approaching educational problems. Both Ben and Sylvia indicated that they were regarded by their fellow teachers as "different." Ben felt that in his student-centered approach he was "more liberalized." Sylvia, in comparing herself with other teachers whom she regarded as traditionally prepared, stated:

I feel infinitely more flexible and am sure they look at me as a radical in a lot of ways because I'm not conventional in the way that they are. I feel better prepared! It comes from flexibility—from not having to stick with the adopted readers because they're the only ones you have dittos for . . . and being able to bring other materials into the classroom. The majority of teachers I see are locked into one set of textbooks, one set of dittos, one set of what you do at P.E. time, and they repeat the thing year after year. There is no way I could begin to survive in that kind of thing. So I feel better prepared, but I also feel that I can't communicate with any of them.

A problem in communication seemed to result from differing perceptions associated with programs of preparation. Sylvia felt that her perspective was different from her traditionally trained colleagues: "We don't share the same interests nor the same feelings about education and kids. They think kids are something to be controlled and disciplined." Ben referred to this perspective as "a frame of reference." He was currently using it, he said, in teaching a parent education class in the evenings.

One way or another, most of the respondents seemed to suggest that the program may be credited for supporting or developing a point of view that they identified with it and that they shared. Maxine called it the "philosophy of children as human beings rather than enemies or objects to be taught." She said that this philosophy "has been integrated into my teaching style." She regarded this as central to the fact that, as a result of the program, she is a different kind of teacher than she might otherwise have been.

Out of the apparent contradictions that characterized their answers to the survey questions, a pattern emerged that gave the participants' responses integrity. The declared importance of the program's philosophy was pitted against a rejection of abstractions: The program was important because it promoted the development of insights and understandings versus the view that experiences *before* or *after* the program were responsible for such development. The synthesizing element involved, however, was a humanistic orientation to which both the program and its participants subscribed. The emphasis was on people—that is, the relationships among them and the ways in which they provide support to one another. The participants seemed to be saying that it was through others that they gained identity and purpose and had their ideas and their actions validated.

For some, the process of validation arose from their ethnic heritage. It predated their participation in the program and was preeminent in its demands upon their energies. For others, the process of validation was heavily dependent upon self-discovery in connection with a continuous and exploratory approach to interpersonal relationships. While musing that her marriage to a fellow participant promised to be the most sustained association, Gail affirmed that she has remained in telephone contact with several who have left the area. "Those friends still provide that important support for what we are all doing," she stated.

The need for professional stimulation and for support in problem solving had been met in the program, many respondents observed. But those whose public school situation provided them with a continuing climate of inspiration and commitment to shared purpose, regarded themselves as especially fortunate. When a stimulating atmosphere was not forthcoming, they sought it elsewhere: in extension courses, in movement to other districts that offered opportunities for professional growth, or in movement away from public school teaching toward lines of endeavor that promised somehow to arouse people and to help them question, grow, and develop. Boyd confessed:

It is just my way to question the old ways. I did respect the "old school marm" next door, but I couldn't abide the price paid for learning—a total dictatorship of the kid. . . . I knew the people in public schools really wouldn't care or want to hear what I knew about kids. But to find out that this was really true began to sap my enthusiasm immensely. I quit the public schools after an extraordinary three years of turbulence. . . . It is important to me to be in a viable alternative education school, now.

Gail commented that since the summer of 1971 she has been frustrated because she receives very little feedback in relation to her in-school activities. She said, "I am also frustrated by a lack of colleagues who will spend time thinking, talking about, and working toward some kind of professional growth." She would like to be around people who share ideas "about what is good for children."

"Nothing seems relevant nor irrelevant of itself—it all depends upon the people involved" is what the participants seemed to be saying. Sylvia recalled the interactions within the group and related these to the needs of teachers. She felt that being able to share ideas and to talk about problems was a help to teachers—that is, it enabled them "to zero in on kids." She was "shocked" to find herself in ". . . a situation in which I get no positive reinforcement, whatsoever . . . except for the kinds of responses that you have to look for in kids and parents to know that you've hit on the right thing." She said that even the administration seems indifferent:

I work for a principal who does nothing. He hasn't even observed me this year, and yet he recommended me for tenure. I find this very frustrating . . . in the sense that I don't think anyone cares. As long as I'm holding down the fort and moving my kids, nobody's going to hassle me. In a way that's good, because I can create some changes in my classroom and do some things that I think are important. But it can get very lonely and frustrating. I can get really depressed about it . . . . Sharing ideas and problems without criticism is very important.

Sylvia felt the kinds of dialogue that were fostered within the program were critical for concerned teachers. She missed it.

Mia, too, talked about "relating" with people who were in the program. "I found that very helpful," she said. "It helped me to understand motivation and to learn about other backgrounds." Flora, however, regretted that "several" of the persons involved in the program did *not* have the same "concerns" as she did. She said she has only sustained an association with participants of her own ethnic background.

Generally, the participants seemed to have a much clearer insight into their own motivations than they had had five years previously. They recognized the fragility of relationships that support a climate in which optimum teaching and learning can occur. The program philosophy they identified as an important "frame of reference" suggested criteria by which they could judge their particular teaching situations; it was one that drew them toward peers with whom they felt a collegial compatibility; it alienated them from others and made them feel isolated in hostile environments.

The idea that "there is no one right answer" seemed to have been assimilated by the participants. Gail valued "the exposure to radical, alternative methods and ideas." She remembered "the *questioning* of everything we saw." And Freddi related this skepticism to an attitude about perceiving human beings as individuals, each of whom is unique. As teachers, they subsequently railed against monolithic solutions to multidimensional problems. The need to question, evaluate, and question again was understood by many of the participants, and they attributed this point of view and their need to exercise it to their different preparation.

Mentioned as an influence that most frustrated their efforts toward personalizing instruction was a double bind imposed by administrative expectations. On the one hand there was the assumption that a significant number of students would perform "at grade level" and that subject matter content would be "covered"; on the other hand there was an expectation that learning be individualized.

Although the participants continued to question practices and motives of those around them, and indeed their own professional behavior, their own purposes do not appear to have changed. Familiar with the "realities of schools" after five years, however, many were more realistic about the strategies needed to make the changes to which they were committed. Some are seeking power within the administrative hierarchy. Others feel that participating in the preparation of new teachers or in political processes through parent and community development will make the most difference. Still others are attempting to make their own classrooms the best possible learning environments for children. A few, disillusioned with "the system," have sought other alternatives and although still concerned with the "human potential," have looked outside of traditional school systems for means to change the lives of children. However, Cal noted that after teaching in four schools in three districts of two different states, he had become aware that his goals in education would never be realized:

They are extremely idealistic. My attempts within my classroom, no matter how well heralded, will make but a small impact on the total spectrum. . . . The real change comes from those who are outside of the classroom. . . . By far the greatest strides toward achieving my goals have come from my participation in various community projects, and not from my teaching assignments. . . . The number of obstacles which seem to be emitted from the administrative hierarchy are at the very least depressing.

Whereas moving into that administrative hierarchy appeared to be the answer for some of the men in the program, two of the women felt that teacher education offered the solution. Freddi declared:

My goals are the same as stated five years ago. However, by being a part of the educational system, I've been able to see clearly the problems associated with reaching my goals. I plan to continue to use the principles and skills learned at Claremont to motivate and encourage students to continue their education. The ultimate problems do not, however, relate directly to my encouragement of students but rather with the instructors of these students. Therefore, if I am ever to become really effective, I must become involved in the teacher training process.

Maxine's aspirations are similar:

Basically, my purposes have remained the same. I want to teach—especially using my Spanish background. I have changed in one area, however. I would like eventually to change more people by being a teacher trainer. As much as I enjoy the classroom, I feel more children can be reached if teachers are trained properly.

She commented that just as the program has helped her fulfill her goals as a teacher, it also ". . . gave me insights to firm up what my goals are now."

The participants remaining committed to classroom teaching appear to have turned their full attention to the children for whom they are responsible. While shunning the criticisms of administrators and a lack of interest among colleagues, they challenge the premise that a teacher cannot make a difference. Believing that public education is worth time and attention, Gail states, "I concentrate on making my own room a good place for children." She never intended, she averred, to work toward change other than "from the inside as a teacher rather than from the outside."

Although Helga has always sought to create an optimum learning environment in her classroom, her idea of "a good place for children" has changed. Ever interested in philosophical and psychological issues, she has come to examine these with an increased respect for the importance of developing social responsibility in children:

I know some adults who are continually unhappy and emotionally upset when they are confronted with having to do something (like earning enough money to eat—or cleaning up after they eat). Our lives are not all free choice. We do have responsibilities.

Whereas she was concerned in the beginning that she not impose her goals upon children, she no longer feels guilty when directing a child's learning activities. Until her students become self-directed and interested in learning and investigating, she teaches them "in a very traditional way, although still using innovative ideas."

While Sylvia once regarded innovative materials and techniques as critical, her views have also changed. She no longer feels that attainment of a good education for children depends upon pedagogical artifacts. Innovative teaching comes from creativity within the person and from association with other creative people. Innovation should be directed toward respecting the rights of children. Whereas Sylvia once felt that reaching out into the community was a way of helping children, she too now focuses on her own classroom:

I've learned to shut my big mouth and do my thing in my room and say very little to anybody about what goes on. And fortunately for me, my kids have done really well academically. Some things are important to fight for and some aren't. I think I've learned what's important to fight for in education. If I stay in it longer (and I may get out of it all together), I may start fighting for it pretty soon. Once I got tenured, I felt much more confident and secure. It helped me out to know that I wasn't stepping on anyone's toes too badly and that I was accomplishing something.

Developing a relationship with each of her children is now uppermost in her mind:

There is little I can do as a person to influence parents' lives or family constellations. My parent contact is very little this year for the first time. I have made no home visits. I've had a better year than I've ever had before, mainly because I was concentrating on the kid as he came into my room . . . and the environment that we supported in my classroom. We would talk about family when it came up but there was no forced situation. I didn't go to any homes and actively engage in rapport building. I concentrated mainly on the child, and parents started coming into my classroom and asking to talk. These conversations with parents were much more beneficial than previously.

Sylvia's thoughts of reaching out to the community to understand children have dissipated in frustration. As a teacher she has chosen to create an optimum environment in the classroom regardless of the environment at home. She no longer feels there are damaging effects on children in trying to "straddle" different environments because ". . . the child is more flexible than we give him credit for." She said:

You can create an environment in the classroom that's completely different as long as you aren't making any judgment about who he is or denigrating where he comes from. The danger is only when the classroom environment comes into conflict with his own. But we can create another environment totally unrelated to what's going on in the street, and he can still succeed because its real for school. You don't have to duplicate the street in the classroom, which I thought you had to do.

Sylvia said that she might change her mind in another year. She felt the program gave her *that* kind of flexibility as well as orienting her toward effecting change in schools.

In spite of many frustrations, as a group the participants reported that they have made substantial changes in their schools. Although a few of them felt that in five years they had changed very little, most reported a sense of competence and confidence about their accomplishments. Achievements have ranged from attitudinal change to the establishment of concrete programs. Staff sentiments relating to ethnically different minorities and to children with special handicaps had been affected. Concrete changes were felt in classrooms, schools, and even in entire systems. In two instances, the activities in which participants became involved related to whole communities.

Among those who perceived themselves as impotent, were Helga, Gail, Clive, and Tina. Optimistically, however, Helga felt that perhaps in the future she might "change things." She spent five years "getting my feet on the ground," she reported. And Gail regretted that the changes she has tried to make "just haven't happened." She noted that "in a situation in which change is too much trouble for all concerned . . . the effort to change is difficult to sustain." She saw her district's "no waves policy" as prevailing until an issue reaches such political intensity that the central office "is forced to examine what's going on." Gail doubted that significant changes can be made by a teacher within the structure of public education:

I used to think I had made changes. I organized many school events—book fairs, programs of mini-courses that involved a lot of parents, etc. Although all of these things were successful and considered important enough to show visitors, etc., I realized recently that none of these things could ever happen again unless I personally caused them to happen. That's not change!

Clive shared Gail's feelings of disillusionment and powerlessness:

I really feel that I have been influential in changing the attitudes and behavior of a specific number of students. However, I have not done one damn thing to make a change in the most important aspects of the public school system because individual teachers just don't have the necessary power to make changes in even one single school. Thus, my desire to become an administrator and at least be able to make some changes on a grander scale than I have been able to.

Clive saw in his classroom many manifestations of contemporary social problems. "Dope, drinking, sex, and 'the dozens'," he noted as just some of the aspects of student's lives that absorbed their attention and diverted their energy. He did not believe that the issues involved were being approached in a way that was either meaningful to students or effective:

One thing I learned from the program was that survival of the student is the most important thing to the student. Because this is the case, there is need to emphasize those things that will enable the student to deal with his social and political surroundings. . . . The need is for teacher awareness of the problems and priorities of students . . . what their needs and desires are. Teachers, I feel, should ask themselves what they are making "real" to their students? Once they are able to grasp the significance of this they will be able to organize and move toward the real solving of real problems confronting their students.

Although in a different way, Tina also hopes that eventually she might make the schooling process a more humane one:

I'd like (in my own school) to be less institutional; I'd like to be working with people who were sharing something together and not just responding to the institution—where you're always aware of board members walking outside your classroom and that sort of thing. I'd like to know that parents believed in what I was doing so that I wouldn't have to pull the wool over their eyes. I like shared commitments.

She claims no interest in ". . . political and administrative games. . . . I think you choose your battles. If your choice is to make a statement to the administration—then fine. But that's not my choice." Tina has left school teaching.

Stu, on the other hand, believes that he will always remain involved in education. While clinging to his goals of five years earlier, he has become "disenchanted" with the means by which he hoped to achieve them. There are too many sources of frustration in the school system itself. Within it he felt more like a clerk, a recordkeeper, and a disciplinarian than a teacher:

There are so many things that are affecting schools today: history, government policies, economic circumstances, television, gang warfare, and the lifestyles of people who are contained within innercities. . . . Sometimes the lifestyles of the students I was working with was also frustrating—lack of initiative, a "gimme" complex, the display culture, a lot of rhetoric, the drugs on the campus—these really slowed down a lot of things that we both could have done together. . . . When you work for the school system, too many of the things you're trying to do are cancelled out, and you waste a lot of energy and burn yourself out.

Stu no longer feels he can effect change by working *for* the schools. He would like to work *with* the schools through large and stronger influences. The media, governmental policy, legislation, and also the private sector have potential, he thinks, for effecting change that he, personally, is unable to do—"not with the layers of bureaucracy that one has to deal with." Stu has come to feel "a sense of despair" at the possibility of effecting important change while working in schools themselves.

Flora and Mia, however, were happy about the way in which they had been able to change the attitudes of teachers concerning the Mexican-American culture. Mia felt that she had a continuous professional impact. In the district in which she first worked, she taught in a model bilingual classroom and then participated in a study of cultural learning styles. Later, when she began teaching in another agricultural community, she was amazed to find that the teachers were referring to Mexican-American children as "Spanish," which she felt was a symptom of deep prejudice and stereotyping. She had helped the teachers, the administration, and even the children themselves to clarify the difference between Chicano and Spanish. She was certain that the children's self-concept and esteem depended upon this clarification:

That was a tremendous input toward change, because here the people at the school kept talking about the self-concept and the self-image of a child, and all the time they kept referring to this kid as "Spanish."

Flora stated:

Attitudes of students, teachers, and administrators have at least been challenged by my steadfast goals. I have reviewed films and books for my district—banning, recommending, etc. I have been active in our A.M.A.E. [Association of Mexican-American Educators] which has changed (politically) various funding and programs for the betterment of our group, in addition to the dominant group.

She regarded as imperative that Anglo teachers become sensitized to the differences of all students and that the expectations for minority students' achievement be no lower than for that of others. They must be prepared to compete academically, she proclaimed, and she indicated that her work had contributed to improved preparation.

Sylvia, along with Stu, reported changes in teacher attitudes about educationally handicapped children. Sylvia explained:

If I've changed the attitude of every teacher in the school about what an EH [educationally handicapped] child is, I did it very methodically. Destructive teachers had damaged children and made them hostile and vengeful. . . . They were considered uncontrollable and unteachable. I worked with the most capable EH children with the idea of mainstreaming them. . . . Now the teachers are beginning to see these kids have something to offer the school and they have talents and can learn. There has been a big change in the teachers in this school.

Cal reportedly affected his colleagues in quite a different way:

If I have made any change, it has been in subtly influencing fellow staff members to defend their professional rights. Most of the teachers that I have worked with in the past four years have been scared of both administrators and school boards. It seems to be inconsistent to me to have people working, guiding, and directing the young, who are essentially afraid of the system of which they are a part.

Boyd reported on independent research that showed his children had made "dramatic gains" in the classroom in spite of slanderous reports to the contrary. "Many parents, however, simply thought kids didn't learn in my room," he stated, and this lack of parent confidence eventually led Boyd to leave public education and to begin teaching in an alternative school.

A number of the participants made changes in school organization. Ben began by teaching an "opportunity class" that most teachers regarded as "a dumping ground for really rough youths." Although he could *teach* these adolescents in isolated circumstances, Ben realized that he could not help them to adjust to the school milieu unless they had regular contact with it. For this reason, he developed the "student growth center" mentioned earlier. In it volunteers from local community colleges gave support to the youths. For this effort he was nominated by his district as an Outstanding Secondary Teacher of America. Subsequently, he became head of the regional juvenile diversion project because of the expanded opportunities it offered him "to make a difference." He felt the project had potential for making "far-reaching changes" in approaches to juvenile problems because it fosters cooperation among schools, police departments, and other community agencies in five cities. Having launched a coordinated policy-making effort among public officials and by getting people involved at all levels, Ben said, "We are seeing a lot of changes in attitudes and feelings." Ben wants to continue working toward a multidimensional attack upon problems inhibiting growth and development among the young.

Stu's interests were similar to Ben's. He created an environmental education program within the district for which he worked. This program was adopted by several other districts. Although these programs continued, Stu is no longer associated with them. He left the public schools to work with youngsters in the federally funded Upward Bound program of which he became associate director. He views this work as having greater potential for impact upon young lives than was offered in public school teaching.

Freddi's change strategies were aimed at the parents of low-income children:

I have been involved with the development of preschool programs in the school district, and with community organizations. I initiated and developed a parent education program. . . . This particular program was designed to provide parents with skills, techniques and methods of working with children at home and at school. This program also provides parents with information as to the kind of schooling their children should be receiving.

Victor, too, had ideas about the kind of schooling that was appropriate to the children in his school community. He was concerned that these Spanish-speaking children be provided with bilingual instruction, instead of merely "a pullout type of program" intended to develop English-as-a-Second-Language (ESL). Victor felt that as his school's ESL instructor, during his first year of teaching, he was influential in the decisions that placed him in the position of a "bilingual teacher" the following year. His own research in the field of biculturalism, plus his capability with the language, gave him a credibility that enhanced his leadership capacities. These capabilities continue to be tapped in the committee work of the district.

Maxine's contribution to change was based directly on her graduate experience. She wrote a paper during her program developing a bilingual-bicultural curriculum. Through her efforts, the school district in which she worked instituted the cross-cultural program she designed. The pilot phase began at the junior high school level and was later expanded to include the elementary school. Also as a direct result of her minischool experience, Maxine suggested to her board of education that each teacher within the district be given a $100 discretionary fund. This suggestion was implemented and has provided teachers with increased decision-making power.

After looking around and comparing themselves with other teachers, none of whom had had the opportunity to create their own schools, most participants in the program felt that their program experiences had affected them deeply. Their professional behavior in schools, as well as activities outside, often differed from those of other educators. The changes they succeeded in effecting varied in both content and style. More profoundly affected, however, was a point of view toward schooling as a social process. Five years had tempered the idealistic expectations they had gained through planning, preparing, and running their minischools. But also, most had become aware of the flexibility and power that the program made available to them with expansion of their professional roles. During those years, they were able to assess more realistically the limitations of that power as well as its magnitude. Confronted with the constraints upon teachers, they became less sanguine about the level of influence actually available to them in the classroom. In response, the schoolmakers have chosen different roads toward the future.

14 Looking Ahead

The experimental Teacher Leader Program described in this study was developed on the premise that change was needed—that past solutions to educational problems were inadequate in the world of the sixties and early seventies and most certainly in the years that lay ahead. While many teacher preparation programs in the late sixties had been developed around concepts of cultural pluralism, in most only the content of the programs reflected a shift from earlier emphases. The project described here was designed in response to a concern that the usual *processes* had been ineffective in sustaining a commitment to improved and appropriate practices.

Underlying the program's structure was a belief that teachers "make a difference,"[a] and that if teachers are to act innovatively, new ways of preparing them needed to be discovered and tested. Its design rested upon assumptions that learning is an active process, that theoretical and experiential learning should be dynamically interrelated, and that differences among students should be encouraged. The curriculum focused upon developing in its participants the flexibility, competence, and power to effect changes in relation to the educational, social, and political circumstances of poor and culturally different children of all ages.

Central to the concept of this program were the small community-based schools—minischools—that the fourteen carefully selected participants created in Southern California during the summer of 1971. In creating the schools, students made all the decisions that go into an educational program: funding, gaining community support, staffing, housing, selecting curriculum, and evaluating the program. Each minischool reflected the neighborhood in which it was established, and each was different in form and content.

Planning for these minischools was the culminating activity of a year's academic work and field experiences. The year's program was designed to foster the understandings and the skills required to provide children with appropriate and effective educational environments. Objectives for the participants stressed an understanding of the culture of poverty and of minority groups, honesty

---

[a] This "belief" has been affirmed in the findings of a recent study in which the data revealed that teachers can contribute to student learning. In fact, the kind of instruction and teaching a student receives is an important predictor of academic achievement. See Frederick J. McDonald, *Beginning Teacher Evaluation Study: Phase II Summary Report.* (Princeton, New Jersey: Educational Testing Service, 1976) pp. 11–12.

in communication, and the ability to identify specific learning needs and to plan curriculum and instructional approaches that would meet those needs. As a result of their first year's experience, the preservice teachers (preterns) were expected to be able to apply their theoretical understanding to local situations, to identify the values, needs, and problems of the culturally different, and to respond to these sensitively and empathically. A basic assumption of the program design was that in the process of planning and running their own minischools, the participants would develop those decision-making and interpersonal skills that are prerequisite to leadership within organizational structures.

A supervised internship year followed in which the participants served as salaried employees in public schools and began to use what they had learned in the program. Thus, they launched their careers as teachers and were expected to serve as educational "change agents" and to exhibit the innovative and creative behaviors associated with the leadership role.

This five-year longitudinal study evaluates the power of the Teacher Leader Program and assesses the viability of transferring its particular characteristics to other teacher preparation projects. Observed, described, and evaluated were the content and processes of the program, the subsequent professional career patterns of the participants, and their reports concerning the interface between themselves, schools, and communities. To determine whether outcomes, both intended and unintended, were enduring, the data were studied in the light of the program's primary purposes. In this final chapter, policy implications are presented regarding the initial and continuing education of teachers as the country enters its third century.

Much of the early data were gathered using participant and participant-observer reports and evaluations. Open-ended surveys and interviews provided the information that was collected after five years had elapsed. While specific issues were targeted for inquiry, the sociological approaches to data gathering increased the likelihood that unanticipated consequences and outcomes might also surface.[b]

---

[b]Participants were given their original statements of purpose to review, and the following questions were asked of them: Did the program help you to accomplish your goals? Since the summer of 1971, what things have contributed to the achievement of these goals? What things have frustrated your efforts? How do you feel about the goals which you had five years ago? Are your purposes the same or different? In what ways? Why? Since leaving the program you probably have come in contact with many traditionally prepared teachers. In what way have you felt better prepared? Less well prepared? Give examples. *As a result of the program*, do you see yourself as a different kind of teacher than you might have otherwise been? Give examples. What aspects of the program were most influential in your subsequent professional behavior? Why? During the course of the program the term "change agent" was frequently used. Do you feel you have changed anything? Knowing what you know now, how do you feel that teachers can be best prepared to make changes in the system? What is there about the schooling process that you would most like to see changed? How do you think this can be accomplished? What do you think you will be doing five years from now? Of the associations created within the program, were any sustained? How have these been significant to you?

Participants were also asked to list and describe all their activities for each year since the program ended: professional positions (title, employing agency, location), and other positions (political, social, volunteer, etc.). Additionally, information was requested about any public recognition they had received (e.g. awards, news items, grants received, etc.).

Although many conclusions and recommendations presented here were first suggested by one or more participants, the authors take full responsibility for the statements and opinions set forth in this last chapter.

Upon analysis of the fifth-year reports from the participants, we concluded that most considered themselves "different" from other teachers with whom they worked in the public schools. There was a constant pressure toward conformity and uniformity, however, that required much inner strength as well as external support to resist. The question among some of the participants was whether resistance was worth the effort. This fostered some movement toward traditionalism. Nonetheless, they still regard themselves as different, and these perceived differences appear to have been both detrimental and beneficial to aspects of their professional lives.

The instructional activities and strategies that were employed and reported by the participants varied widely. These differences might be attributed to the heterogeneity of the group, as well as to a philosophical orientation engendered by the program that solutions are a function of situations. Such a viewpoint, while freeing participants to consider alternatives among educational possibilities, also deprived them of the certainty that accompanies teaching by formula. Perhaps as a consequence almost all participants reported generally low morale. They felt alienated from their peers and frustrated by administrative indifference. Perceiving their professional environments as hostile, and dissatisfied with the lack of choices available to them as classroom teachers, a few have left teaching. Others are looking toward alternative career patterns that hold potential, they believe, for heightening their influence as advocates of change. The number of different career paths taken by the group of fourteen who completed the program seems much greater than expected for such a small number of new teachers.

Although the sentiments of individual participants disposed them to focus attention upon different societal subgroups and different aged children, they were all committed to equalizing educational opportunities. Whether or not the program incrementally affected that commitment is a question that remains unanswered. However, most participants seemed to feel that the program provided them with the *means* of fulfilling their commitment—that is, it extended their understandings and supplied them with strategies for change. A few credited the program with nothing more than personal compatibility: It legitimized their own inclinations and made possible implementing ideas that otherwise might not have reached fruition.

The overall goal of the program, as implied in its title, was to produce teachers who were committed to finding solutions to the educational inequities consequent to cultural and economic differences. Although in a nonquantitative study determining with precision the variables most influential toward achievement of the program's mission is difficult, we can make some judgments by comparing the purposes of the program with the evidence accumulated. The data collected are therefore examined in the light of questions about the development in participants of those skills, attitudes, and understandings the program was designed to foster.

Did the program create teachers responsive to the needs and aspirations of the poor and culturally different?

Because the selection committee sought teacher candidates who were already concerned with the human predicament, stating that the program "created" compassionate, empathic teachers is not possible. It did, however, create a climate that sustained this point of view and allowed the participants an opportunity to exercise their basic humanness in multicultural settings.

When developing their minischools, the participants had to be sensitive to community needs. In many cases, the ideas that seemed helpful to them in teaching the community's children were not always accepted with trust by the children's parents. A process of mutual accommodation among residents and participants increased the respect of each for the other's ideas. Therefore, the participants' regard for community members, not as objects of experimentation but as partners in the process of problem solving, was reinforced.

Although solutions varied, one aspect remained constant. Each group allied itself with an organized effort offering hope that aspects of their minischool might be sustained. No program was totally independent of community-based or institutionally-based interest. There were no independent "store-front" schools, as one might have expected. The participants wanted to succeed, but they were wary of creating minischools as "hit-and-run ego-trips" for themselves. Nor did they want to be perceived as "do-gooders." A really successful minischool, they all agreed, would be one that was self-perpetuating because of ecological validity.

Since participants were selected who were committed to working with "the disadvantaged," the investigators were interested in determining what portion of the group remained active in this regard after a five-year period. Approximately two-thirds of the participants continued to be involved with problems relating to the disenfranchised, although a number of them were no longer in the classroom.

Did the program develop special skills for working with the poor and powerless?

The most compelling evidence that the program did achieve this purpose is found in the records of the minischools. The organization, content, and the target population of each minischool was different. That these were appropriately related may be judged by the level of community participation, since attendance at the minischools was voluntary. In most cases it remained at original levels or increased during the period of the schools' operation.

The participants unanimously attributed to their minischool experiences those learnings that at the time were most salient and have been most significant to them in terms of their preparation for specialized teaching and their subsequent professional activities and responsibilities. However, while they were freer to work *with* students rather than against them—while they were freer to discover their own styles and to develop and hone them—there was a price the participants paid: The program was costly in time and required a heavy toll in terms of anxiety. All the experiences the participants most valued in the acquisition of skills were, like the minischools, ones they sought out for themselves in response to individually perceived problems. Experiences the program designers preplanned because they seemed logically and theoretically relevant to the program's mission were not always considered worthy of time, thought, and commitment by those in the program. The program component that was called a Learning Community, is one example of prestructuring that although an essentially attractive idea to program designers, was not at the time seductive to the participants. They were not psychologically ready to join together for the purpose of identifying areas of common concern and of initiating the action upon which solutions might depend. However, after five years, some who did not recognize the value of this peer support system that was available to them during the program acknowledged that the concept had merit. Some even went so far as to suggest the value of adapting the idea to their current professional circumstances.

Did the program create teachers who were generators of new ideas and initiators of action? Did the program develop change-agents?

If the program created effective professionals, minischools were most responsible for that outcome. The minischools were action-oriented and varied in their innovative qualities. They were built upon the decision-making powers of the participants, which were sharpened through discussion, compromise, and reevaluation. The exercise of these powers enabled the participants to discover their own professional identities and fostered autonomy, rather than dependency. Nothing in their minischools was predetermined: not goals, not curricula, not the structure of programs. Each aspect of each minischool required rational assessment and planning by the preterns. The process of thinking through, developing, justifying, clarifying, and implementing their ideas in a *total* program required that the participants assume many roles and begin to crystallize personal philosophies of education as they made the hard decisions for which *they* necessarily assumed responsibility. In some cases, they even sought and gained access to policymakers within school bureaucracies, which is a strategy that is hardly conceivable to the ordinary teacher.

Accountable only to their own commitments, each task group had to create its own indicia of success without the security of feedback from institutional superordinates or from others standing in professional judgment. With such an introductory experience, the participants seem to have grown comparatively resistant to the socialization processes to which many traditionally prepared teachers succumb. It provided them with a broad perspective on problems, as well as an awareness of the premises that underlie educational programs. They felt that the program enabled them to evaluate school practices and to resist or to circumvent, at least in part, those that seemed inappropriate.

In 1971, what did seem appropriate to the participants was a genuine involvement by parents and community people in the process of schooling. There was a predictable consistency among the preterns regarding this concern, and many still emphasized its importance after five years had elapsed. Their commitment to the concept of local control in schooling is probably not surprising since all of them vigorously sought means to control their own educational destinies.

The assumption that a program is most effective when the people affected by it are part of the planning process was confirmed in the evolution of the Teacher Leader Program generally and in the minischools in particular. Perhaps the most important finding of this study is that as a result of the program, three interrelated qualities were developed that characterized the participants' professional behavior and elevated it above that of the fungible teacher: autonomy, responsibility, and accountability. Throughout the data there appear reports that the program, by requiring its participants to formulate, effect, and defend their own educational programs, fostered in them professional strengths that made them more than interchangeable parts in a system. The participants' decisions relating to their minischool programs were made in quite different ways and depended upon individual or group points of departure as well. But regardless of the starting point, the participants confronted one problem that is shared by all who are concerned with the teaching and learning process— that is, the problem of how to avoid developing dependency and how to allow autonomy when it may result in student behavior that is contrary to what is valued and sought.

This problem was also highlighted at the graduate level in another aspect of the program. As part of their field experience, the preterns were encouraged to explore circumstances in communities and schools that they saw as relevant to their particular concerns. They were expected to identify for themselves situations that provided individually appropriate learning opportunities. The openness of such a program structure not only created anxiety within the group, it also raised questions among supervising faculty when a participant's perceptions diverged radically from their own. Additionally, it created interpersonal tension because of some participants' perceptions that the program was "vague" and without definition at the same time that unarticulated expectations existed.

There were times during the course of the program when the preterns showed that they equated its nondirectiveness with a lack of form or content. This view was expressed in hostility toward the program's creators and administrators. However, many participants later saw the openness they had experienced as a beneficial attribute of the program and regarded it as a necessary humanistic condition for educational activities. The philosophy that supported personalization in teaching and learning became woven into the fabric of their own professional behavior, and while several participants acknowledged the source of their assumptions, others seemed not to recognize relationships with the program.

In a study that depends heavily on self-report by the participants, their failure to perceive a phenomenon does not mean it did not exist. It does mean that the study is limited in its ability to document outcomes about which the authors have little doubt and much subjective evidence. Acquainted with the participants since they entered the program, the investigators observed numerous signs of knowledge, understandings, and skills gained by the preterns. Some of it became so well integrated into the participants' systems that they appeared to have no awareness that it may not have originated with them. For learners to claim the teacher's ideas for their own is the kind of bittersweet reward to which good educators aspire.

There was, after five years, a corollary compensation in the credit that participants gave the program for the learning they did in minischools and in other self-selected experiences. The participants regarded these as the most valuable experiences enjoyed during the time they were preparing to become teachers. However, they did not regard activities they initiated as associated with "the program." If teacher educators wish to protect their credibility and their delicate egos, they should most certainly make explicit the unifying principles and underlying rationales that guide their teaching. They should state clearly the extent to which their programs model the practices they espouse. A recommendation of the investigators is that educational programs reflect a delicate balance between predetermined (logically sequenced) experiences and self-selected (psychologically sequenced) experiences.

Aside from pedagogical reasons for prestructuring some of the learning experiences provided for teacher candidates, there may also be practical constraints that guide the choice of activities and the time frame in which they are offered. If possible, minischools of variable lengths, planned in accordance with the objectives of participants, might prove more effective. These could be expected to better complement the learning and teaching styles of individual program participants as well as the needs of the communities.

The continuing development of the participants' decision-making capacities has depended upon the school situations in which they have found themselves. Those who received administrative support and therefore perceived themselves as able to influence people, programs, and policies have done so. Innovations such as bilingual curricula, parent education projects, transition classes for adolescents, and other alternative school models and practices have suggested the multiplier effect the program developers intended. Others reported that their school environments seemed inhospitable to new ideas and innovative activity and that they missed the support system provided by the program.

The academics of the program enabled many to understand intellectually the dynamics involved when one tries to alter the status quo. From both negative and positive experiences in the field, the participants *began* to understand the forces set in motion that militated against change. However, they were generally unprepared for the resistances and the restraints they encountered in real-life stiuations. As a result, some report employing adaptive coping strategies and covert means of working toward their goals, rather than risk suppression through attention-getting behavior. The data do not reveal whether those who have postponed attempting to make changes outside their classrooms will indeed alter their behavior upon attaining the level of security sought. They do, however, show that after five years, the participants all communicate a heightened cynicism about the possibility of effecting a wide-ranging change in the schools. The program's intent to foster optimistic attitudes among new teachers was not fulfilled. Additionally, the program's intent to create change agents needs critical analysis.

While intended to develop "leaders" and "change agents," a major shortcoming of the program's design was that these terms were never precisely defined. At no time did the program's developers describe explicitly the arena in which "leaders" were expected to function. At no time were the specific changes described that the leaders were supposed to effect, nor was the level identified at which changes were expected to occur. The teacher leaders were expected to discover the sources of educational problems and then to bring their skills to bear in the service of solutions that would in turn affect social relationships.

That change occurs at three levels—instructional, institutional, and societal— was assumed. Another assumption was that through a ripple effect, change initiated at one level would impact impressively upon circumstances at other levels. This assumption was not defined operationally, nor was it explicitly targeted for examination.

The study does reveal that changes reported as having begun within the classroom—at the instructional level—have had little effect upon the structure and directions taken by the participants' institutions. Those changes that participants effected at the institutional level were by and large a result of effort exerted when "the teacher leaders" extended their range of activities beyond the institutional role.

The teacher's role, as traditionally defined, offers extremely limited opportunity for effecting change, except as "change" is related to the quality of life *within* the classroom and the impact it has directly upon the lives of children. Although such intraclassroom change may be a laudable goal, questions must be asked relative to the cost effectiveness of special programs if their purposes do not extend beyond those shared with all other teacher education programs. On the other hand, during periods of declining enrollment and limited demand for new teachers, there exists opportunity for reallocation of resources toward the creation of a cadre of instructional specialists who have credibility with other teachers and the ability to influence them as informed peers, not hierarchical supervisors.

Did the program enable its participants to make schools sources of trust, and instruments of cultural democracy?

The communities' responses to the diverse minischools were evidence that these programs were congruent with community needs. The little schools developed the commitment of both children and adults within the neighborhoods they served.

In retrospect, the program's entire curriculum—extensive community explorations, intensive self-selected schools practica, the peer learning community, academic course work including electives in ethnic studies, and especially the minischools—combined to develop in participants a multicultural perspective. Such an enlarged view of the components of human society heightened their sensitivity to individual needs. This sensitivity was particularly apparent in the climate of the minischools where the posture of adults toward children and young people reflected a multidimensional approach to role relationships and a respect for the personhood of each learner. Having visited children in their homes and welcomed both parents and siblings into their minischools, most participants were wary of erecting status barriers; both children and teachers related to each other as human beings rather than as objects to be manipulated.

Experiences in the community—including both practica and minischools—fostered in the participants an appreciation for the importance of teachers enjoying positive and informed relationships with their school communities. These experiences reinforced a commitment to the inclusion of the school's clientele in the policy-making process.

The heterogeneity of the group of teacher aspirants was identified by some participants as a microcosm of cultural democracy and therefore a rich program resource. It seemed more appreciated five years later than it was at the time they were together. In retrospect, their varied viewpoints were regarded as aiding in the development of social understandings associated with the motivational aspects of teaching and learning.

Upon analysis, the Teacher Leader Program appears to have been instrumental in preparing a different kind of teacher. The teachers produced seemed especially competent in working with the poor; they had special skills for working with the culturally different. Although many participants went into the public schools with new ideas, their ability to implement them depended upon the organization and the structure of the schools in which they found themselves. The power to make schools sources of trust and instruments of cultural democracy will, of course, depend upon more than a few students in an experimental program. Nonetheless, outcomes of this experiment suggest alternatives to many preservice practices current among teacher training programs.

Underlying all learning opportunities planned for the Teacher Leader Program was the intent to make new teachers responsible for their own professional development, as well as the intellectual, emotional, and social growth of children preparing to live within a cultural democracy. Aspects of the program to which such outcomes may be attributed are those that especially characterized it and distinguished it from traditional programs of teacher preparation. These include: self-selected academic and experiential learning opportunities; a peer learning community; and most importantly, the minischools. All of these may be incorporated into programs of teacher preparation and development. Of course, for preservice programs, the implications are profound with regard to state certification requirements. Also, such programs' effectiveness in other settings, other times, other social contexts, and with other participants is a question that remains to be answered.

Examining the experiences of the participants during the five years since their minischools makes it apparent that constant professional growth must be encouraged if the ubiquitous pull toward conformity is to be overcome. Just as new modes of preservice preparation are indicated if teachers are to grow in the varied ways required by a pluralistic society, inservice education must offer multidirectional opportunities also. Some of the learning experiences that seem appropriate to the goals of preservice programs might be adapted to the benefit of the practicing teacher. Summer projects that, like the minischools, are characterized by diversity and openness to the unexpected might offer rich opportunities for teachers to learn along with the children for whom the programs are designed. Self-selected learning experiences promise opportunities for self-discovery in relation to problems that require identification. The outcomes of heuristic methods are often the more valuable because they may not be precisely identified in advance. Through exploratory processes, teachers may acquire the set required when planning *for* change takes precedence over the linear "planned change."

The grassroots impetus toward "teacher centers" reveals the attraction of peer learning communities. When colleagues can find ways to work together for purposes of mutual support, evaluation becomes a self-correcting mechanism toward growth, rather than a threat to professional survival. Such growth can be enriched by the continued participation of institutions of higher education to the extent that their involvement is more clinical than judgmental. Individually or together, in small groups or large, teachers who assume responsibility for their own development are exercising powers of decision making. Ultimately, this power characterizes them as professionals, instead of merely instructional technicians. However, true professionals, willing to be autonomous and accountable, require an institutional environment in which they are allowed to exercise their powers if these are to develop fully. The attempt to analyze the program's effects upon the subsequent professional behavior of the participants made it apparent that the problem was confounded by forces exerted within the school districts in which participants found themselves. The restraints or encouragements—whether real or imagined, whether from superordinate administrators or from peers—were powerful influences upon the morale and creativity required for professional growth. The consequences of risk taking appeared too great in most cases. To flourish professionally, teachers not only need the personal support of sympathetic human beings, they also need to have their institutional roles redefined or expanded. This process will require drastic reformation of institutional structures and new loci for decisions.

A major finding of this study is that teachers are unable to effect change outside of their classrooms as long as their activities are circumscribed by the instructional role. As classroom teachers confronted with a need for systemic change, the participants felt impotent to control their own destinies. Consequently they experienced frustration—an emotion that teachers historically have shared with minorities, children, and other powerless groups.

The press for change appears most forcefully now at the societal level. Through their legislatures and the courts, the people are demanding responsive schooling. Some states are beginning to acknowledge and act upon a need to reform public education in order to make good the promises implied in schooling for each person involved in it. The new mandate will require new structures and new levels of authority built upon expertise rather than status. As the mandate is acted upon and the complex relationships that affect instruction are recognized, teachers will not simply be freed to function beyond the parameters of traditional roles. Rather, they will be *expected* to exercise a positive influence upon many of the variables critical to the educational outcomes desired.

California's efforts toward school reform are a case in point. Changes proposed (Early Childhood Education, the Master Plan for Special Education, or the Reform of Intermediate and Secondary Education—RISE) are basic to the way schools operate. Other changes, such as desegregation and multicultural and multilingual instruction, are mandated by the courts and demand radical restructuring of institutions. These require teachers who can work with communities, develop curricula, and allocate resources, all of which are new expectations for school teachers. They suggest levels of responsibility for which traditional preservice programs have not prepared them. To be confronted with such expectations without adequate preparation is a frightening and traumatic experience. Those involved in the development of teachers may benefit from knowing about the experiences of the schoolmakers.

Notes

Notes

Chapter 1
The Challenge to Change

1. Omar Grine, "America Against Itself: A Case of Democratic Anarchism?" *Daedalus* 101 (Fall 1972): 104.

2. Arthur Schlesinger, Jr., "The Modern Consciousness and the Winged Chariot," in *Revolutionary Directions in Intellectual and Cultural Productions* (New York: Research Foundation of the City University of New York, 1975), p. 10.

3. See, for example, J. M. Cooper, W. A. Weber, and C. Johnson, *Competency-Based Teacher Education: A Systems Approach to Program Design* (Berkeley, Calif.: McCutchan Publishing Corporation, 1973); Roger A. Kaufman, *Educational System Planning* (Englewood Cliffs, N.J.: Prentice Hall, 1972); Robert F. Mager, *Preparing Instructional Objectives* (Palo Alto, Calif.: Fearon Publishers, 1962); Ralph W. Tyler, *Basic Principles of Curriculum and Instruction* (Chicago: University of Chicago Press, 1950).

4. Willard W. Waller, *The Sociology of Teaching* (New York: Russell and Russell, 1961).

5. Dan C. Lortie, *Schoolteacher* (Chicago: The University of Chicago Press, 1975).

6. Some additional references related to this topic of teacher socialization are as follows: Robert Dreeben, "The School as a Workplace," in R. M. Travers (ed.), *Second Handbook of Research on Teaching* (Chicago: Rand McNally and Company, 1973), pp. 450-73; Elizabeth M. Eddy, *Becoming a Teacher* (New York: Teachers College Press, 1969); D. E. Edgar and R. L. Warren, "Power and Autonomy in Teacher Socialization," *Sociology of Education* 42 (1969): 386-99; Dan C. Lortie, "Teacher Socialization: The Robinson Crusoe Model," in *The Real World of the Beginning Teacher,* Report of the Nineteenth National TERS Conference (Washington, D.C.: National Education Association, 1966), pp. 1-53; William G. Spady, "Teacher Socialization and Vulnerability," *California Journal of Teacher Education* 2, 4 (Spring 1975): 1-20. Also, the work of W. K. Hoy seems especially relevant to this topic: "Organizational Socialization: The Student Teacher and Pupil Control Ideology," *Journal of Educational Research* 61 (1967): 153-55; "Influence of Experience on the Beginning Teacher," *School Review* 76 (1968): 312-23; "Pupil Control Ideology and Organizational Socialization: A Further Examination of the Influence of Experience on the Beginning Teacher," *School Review* 77 (1969): 257-65.

7. Laurence Iannaccone and H. Warren Button, *Functions of Student Teaching: Attitude Formation and Initiation in Elementary Student Teaching* (St. Louis, Mo.: Washington University, 1964).

8. The project, "Program to Develop Teacher Leaders Specializing in the Problems of the Disadvantaged," was funded through the Education Professions Development Act (United States Office of Education). It was developed and carried out at the Claremont Graduate School, Claremont, Calif.

9. See, for example, Malcolm M. Provus, *The Grand Experiment* (Berkeley, Calif.: McCutchan Publishing Corporation, 1975).

10. Christopher Jencks et al., *Inequality: A Reassessment of the Effect of Family and Schooling in America* (New York: Basic Books, 1972).

11. James E. Allen, Jr., "The Federal Role in Teacher Education," in Esther D. Hamsin (ed.), *Realignments for Teacher Education,* Yearbook of the American Association of Colleges for Teacher Education (Washington, D.C.: AACTE, 1970), p. 62.

12. Eddy, *Becoming a Teacher,* p. 120.

13. W. W. Charters, Jr., "The Social Background of Teaching," in N. L. Gage (ed.), *Handbook of Research on Teaching* (Chicago: Rand McNally, 1963), pp. 749-52.

14. Charles E. Silberman, *Crisis in the Classroom: The Remaking of American Education* (New York: Random House, 1970), p. 379.

15. Robert Rosenthal and Lenore F. Jacobson, "Teacher Expectation for the Disadvantaged," *Scientific American* 218 (April 1968): 16, 19-23.

16. James S. Coleman, "The Concept of Educational Opportunity," in *Equal Educational Opportunity,* ed. by the Editorial Board of the *Harvard Educational Review* (Cambridge, Mass.: Harvard University Press, 1969), pp. 20-21.

17. Research and Policy Committee, *Education for the Urban Disadvantaged: from Preschool to Employment* (New York: Committee for Economic Development, March 1971), p. 50.

18. Martin Deutsch, "The Role of Social Class in Language Development and Cognition," *American Journal of Othopsychiatry* XXV (January 1965): 86.

Chapter 4
Getting Ready

1. B. J. Barnes, "The Teacher Leaders: An Heuristically Approached Study of a Preparatory Process in Teacher Education." Ph.D. Dissertation, Claremont Graduate School, Claremont, Calif., 1973.

Chapter 5
Large Tasks for Little Schools

1. For further discussion of these issues see Barnes, "The Teacher Leaders", 1973.

Chapter 11
The Urban Studies Workshop

1.   John Dewey, *Experience and Education* (New York: The Macmillan Company, 1938), p. 78.

2.   Lawrence A. Cremin, *The Transformation of The School* (New York: Alfred A. Knopf, 1962), pp. 333–34.

Chapter 12
Looking Back

1.   Lortie, in his sociological study, states that it is ". . . useful to limit one's control over responses; . . . open-ended inquiry . . . lets teachers describe their world in their language." Dan C. Lortie, *Schoolteacher* (Chicago: University of Chicago Press, 1975), p. 9.

Index

Afro-Americans. *See* Blacks
Aides. *See* Minischool, staff
Anthropology, 37
Anxiety, 46, 49, 51, 52, 55, 56, 139,
    160, 163, 164, 167, 169, 176–
    177, 178, 183; at Black School,
    74; La Escuelita, 76, 82–83; Las
    Palmas, 93, 95; Live Oak, 59;
    Urban Studies Workshop, 122, 128
Art, 54; at La Escuelita, 78, 87, 91;
    at Las Palmas, 98; at Live Oak,
    63, 64; at Ramona, 114; at
    Urban Studies Workshop, 130
Arts and crafts, at Las Palmas, 101; at
    Ramona, 113

Barrio. *See* Community
Ben (participant), 17–18; on black
    education, 40; career of, 155,
    156, 170–171; practicum of,
    48; on program, 141–142, 151,
    158–159, 162; and Urban
    Studies Workshop, 119–135
    passim
Bilingual-bicultural education, 21–22,
    26, 45, 52, 115, 145, 156, 157,
    160, 169, 171; at La Escuelita,
    77, 82, 84, 85, 86, 89–90; at
    Las Palmas, 106; at Ramona, 115
Biculturalism, 21, 76, 78, 79, 80, 171
Bilingualism, 21, 25, 99, 140, 156, 171;
    at La Escuelita, 77, 78, 79; at
    Ramona, 111–112, 115
Blacks, 29, 38, 42, 52, 80, 97; in-
    justices to, 40–41; studied, 39;
    participants on, 40–41, 47, 61,
    68–71; participants' relationships
    with, 49, 93–95, 97; and Urban
    Studies Workshop, 119–120
Black School, 29, 56, 67–74, 148;
    facilities, 71–72; participant's
    evaluation of, 74
Black studies, 39, 69, 71, 72, 73
Boyd (participant), 25–26; career of,
    157, 170; and Las Palmas,
    93–108 *passim;* practicum of,
    49; on program, 146, 152, 153,
    159, 161; on public schools, 163

Cal (participant), 29–30; and Black
    School, 67–74 *passim;* career of,
    158–165; practicum of, 46, 48;
    on program, 151; relations with
    students, 147–148; on United
    States, 40–41
Carpentry, at Ramona, 113, 114

Change: agents of, 4, 11, 12, 17, 45,
    156, 167–172 *passim,* 174, 177,
    180; concepts of, 5, 6, 12, 18,
    168, 182; constraints upon, 12,
    151, 164, 167–169, 170, 174,
    179–180; mandates for, 183;
    need for, 4–7, 11, 18, 20–22,
    24, 28, 40–41, 173, 183; process
    of, 182–183; strategies for, 13,
    26, 28, 30, 37, 110, 111, 125,
    126, 127, 164–165, 175, 176,
    177, 179; in teaching methods,
    159, 166–167, 179, 183. *See
    also* Strategies, instructional
Chicanoism, 78, 79, 140
Chicanos, 19, 38, 39, 42, 44, 52,
    169; injustices to, 41; and La
    Escuelita, 76–91 *passim,* 144;
    and Las Palmas, 96, 97, 99,
    107; participants relations with,
    49, 152; and Ramona, 109;
    teachers of, 150, 152; and Urban
    Studies Workshop, 120
Clive (participant), 17, 19; on black
    education, 40; career of, 155,
    168; on program, 141, 142,
    152, 159; and Urban Studies
    Workshop, 119–135 *passim*
Coleman Report, 6
Communication, 23, 28, 52, 162; at
    La Escuelita, 77, 78, 86, 90; at
    Las Palmas, 93–94, 97, 98, 99,
    100, 101, 104, 105–106, 107;
    program emphasis on, 14, 31,
    32, 36, 38; at Ramona, 112, 114;
    at Urban Studies Workshop, 120,
    121, 125, 129–130, 131
Community, 149, 176, 177–178, 181;
    Ben's work in, 156; of Black
    School, 71; candidates work in,
    39, 43, 44, 45; involvement of,
    11, 23, 24, 26, 37, 52, 176, 177,
    181; of La Escuelita, 76, 78,
    79–80, 82, 83; of Las Palmas,
    96–108 *passim;* of Live Oak, 60;
    and participants, 141, 146–147,
    148, 152, 153, 166–167; pro-
    gram emphasis on 44–45, 52,
    53; of Ramona, 109–110, 114,
    118; understanding of, 12, 14,
    45, 53, 141, 181; and Urban
    Studies Workshop, 120, 121,
    123, 124, 125, 127, 132
Contracting, 54–55
Cooking, at Las Palmas, 107; at
    Ramona, 113, 114, 117;

191

About the Authors

Carolyn Lipton Ellner is associate dean of the Claremont Graduate School and associate professor of education. Working on both coasts, she has been a teacher, principal, and staff developer, as well as director of teacher education at the Claremont Graduate School. She received the B.A. in Philosophy from Mount Holyoke College, the M.A. from Columbia Teachers College, and the Ph.D. with distinction from the University of California, Los Angeles. Dean Ellner currently serves on several boards in California dealing with educational matters as well as broader governmental issues.

B. J. Barnes has been involved in teacher education for the past ten years. She worked closely with the schoolmakers whose activities are described in this book. With the B.A. from Pomona College, she earned both her master's and Ph.D. degrees at the Claremont Graduate School. Since 1972 she has been a member of the education faculty at California State University, Fullerton, where she has served as Coordinator for Elementary Education.